SENATE......

SPECIAL REPORT

ON

PRISONS AND PRISON DISCIPLINE,

MADE UNDER AUTHORITY OF THE

BOARD OF STATE CHARITIES.

By THE SECRETARY OF THE BOARD.

BOSTON:
WRIGHT & POTTER, STATE PRINTERS,
No. 4 SPRING LANE.
1865.

CONTENTS.

	Pages
INTRODUCTORY,	4–7

PART FIRST.
THE VARIOUS SYSTEMS OF PRISON DISCIPLINE, ... 7–52

PART SECOND.
THE MASSACHUSETTS SYSTEM AND ITS RESULTS, ... 53–84

PART THIRD.
PRISON STATISTICS OF MASSACHUSETTS FOR 1864, ... 85–123

APPENDIX.

A,	125–133
B,	134–136
C,	137–138
D,	139
INDEX,	140

Commonwealth of Massachusetts.

EXECUTIVE DEPARTMENT, BOSTON,
March 2, 1865,

To the Honorable the Senate:

I transmit herewith, for the information of the general court, a Report to this department, from the Board of State Charities, prepared by the Secretary of the Board, on the subject of Prisons and Prison Discipline.

The subject to which it relates, and the precise topics it discusses, are alike interesting and important. The Report is made in conformity with the 4th section of the 240th chapter of the Acts of 1863, which provides that the Board "shall investigate and supervise the whole system of the public charitable and correctional institutions of the Commonwealth, and shall recommend such changes and additional provisions as they may deem necessary for their economical and efficient administration."

On perceiving that it contains suggestions which would require legislative consideration in order to render them effectual, and that it contains facts, arguments, and statistics which it is desirable should be within the reach of the general court, and in a convenient form for perusal, I have decided to lay it before your honorable body without the delay which would be incident to a previous complete examination on my own part.

JOHN A. ANDREW.

Commonwealth of Massachusetts.

To His Excellency the Governor and the Honorable Senate :

The undersigned, Secretary of the Board of State Charities, has the honor to submit the following Report on the special subject of Prisons and Prison Discipline.

F. B. SANBORN,
Secretary of the Board of State Charities.

SPECIAL REPORT

ON

PRISONS AND PRISON DISCIPLINE.

At a regular meeting of the Board of State Charities, on the 4th of January, 1865, it was

Voted, "That the Secretary have authority to prepare and present to the Governor a Report on Prisons, Prison Statistics, and Prison Discipline, separate and distinct from his First Annual Report to the Board, already submitted."

My reason for requesting this permission was, that I had collected much information concerning the number, employment, discipline and expense of the prisoners in the Jails, Houses of Correction and State Prison, which could not be well incorporated in my Annual Report, on account of its great length, and which related also to questions not much examined or discussed by the Board. It seemed to me proper, therefore, that whatever statements and suggestions I might make, should stand apart from the recommendations of the Board, until they had found time to examine them, while, at the same time, the importance of the subject was such that they ought also to be communicated to the legislature at the present session.

The natural arrangement of my Report would require, first, a statement of the condition and results of our own prisons, and then a comparison of them with the prisons of other States and countries. But for what appears to me a good reason, I ·shall take the liberty to reverse this order of arrangement, and shall first exhibit the systems of Prison Discipline hitherto in vogue in this State and country; then describe a system entirely new and almost unknown here, which has, for eight years, prevailed in Ireland, with very happy results; and finally, set forth the actual results and condition of our own prison system at present, with some suggestions for its modification. In this way I shall present to those who read (as I trust,) such an order of treatment as may secure a greater interest in the subject, than could be expected from a dry detail of figures introduced at the outset.

PART FIRST.

THE VARIOUS SYSTEMS OF PRISON DISCIPLINE.

The commencement of anything like a theory of Prison Discipline, as most men know, was made by the celebrated HOWARD, about the beginning of our war of the Revolution. His associates and sympathizers were Sir William Blackstone, the eminent jurist, and Sir Frederick Eden, a distinguished writer on pauperism; but little immediate result followed the labors of these three philanthropists. In 1787 the question was taken up by the Society of Friends, in Philadelphia, and about the same time by Sir George Paul, a benevolent magistrate in Gloucestershire, England. In both countries prisons were built, in which the main idea was to separate the prisoners from each other, and to employ them in steady labor. But these prisons very imperfectly realized this idea; solitary confinement might be nominally the rule, but, as Judge Quincy declared of our State Prison in 1822, it was really the exception. Accordingly, experiments were tried of solitary confinement *without labor*, since it was found that the prisons already built were of little value in checking crime or reforming criminals. The first of these experiments in America seems to have been at Auburn, New York, in 1821-22; but it was repeated in Maine, New Jersey and Virginia. In all these instances, it signally failed, and was soon abandoned, for it was found that either the health, the reason, or the moral nature of the convict was ruined by a system so inhuman. From this failure at Auburn sprung what has since been known as the *Auburn System*, but which I have called the *Congregate System*, following in this the felicitous language of Messrs. Howe and Sumner. The peculiarity of this system is that the convicts shall labor in congregation or *association*, as the English term it; at

Auburn, also, they take their meals together, but generally speaking, wherever this system prevails, they are separated during their meals, and at night. That is the system which nominally prevails in all our prisons in Massachusetts; though it is greatly moderated at the State Prison, upon principle, and in the county prisons from accidental causes. Theoretically it involves entire silence on the part of the prisoners towards each other, and hence is sometimes called the *silent* system. But this feature of it is seldom very fully enforced.

While the authorities at Auburn were elaborating their new system of partial separation, the Philadelphia authorities were establishing complete separation among prisoners in their new penitentiary, which was opened for the reception of convicts in 1829, the same year that our State Prison was completed on the Auburn model. Solitary imprisonment *without labor* having been tried in Pennsylvania, as well as at Auburn, without success, it was resolved to introduce labor into the separate prisons, and this policy has been acted upon ever since, in that State.

So distinguished was the success of both these systems,—that of Auburn and that of Pennsylvania,—when compared with the old modes of prison management, that they attracted great notice in Europe, where the matter had received less attention up to 1830. Several commissioners were sent to the United States, between 1830 and 1840, expressly to investigate the American penitentiaries, and the reports of these able commissioners are still high authority on the points then investigated. The inquiries of MM. Beaumont, De Tocqueville, and Demetz, on behalf of the French, and of Mr. Crawford, of the English governments, threw much light on our systems, and were of great service in establishing the modern prisons of France and England. Prussia also sent out a commissioner to examine the same question, and the government of Belgium availed itself of the labors of so many careful observers.

The general voice of these foreign authorities, contrary to American expectation, was for the *separate* or Pennsylvania system. Accordingly, the English and French prisons were generally made to conform to this model. The great penitentiary at Pentonville was built on the Philadelphia plan in 1842. Earlier in the same year, one on the same plan was opened at Perth, and others were established before 1847. At that time, however, and for several succeeding years, the expediency of the Separate System was greatly called in question in England, and in correction of some of its evils,—perhaps, also, as a sort of compromise with the advocates of the Congregate System,—a new, or eclectic system was devised. The first part of a prisoner's sentence was to be passed in separate confinement, but he was then to be transferred to a congregate prison, and put at labor with hundreds of others on public works.

It is at this point that the experience of American and of British prisons parts company. Up to 1850 they had moved along mainly in the same grooves, though there was a considerable superiority in administration and in results in favor of our own prisons. But since 1850, that is, for more than a dozen years, while great improvements have been made in England and Ireland, especially in Ireland, little or nothing has been done here, except by the individual exertions of a few prison officers.

It is to this state of things that I wish to call the attention of the General Court of Massachusetts, for I believe that we have here the opportunity of carrying out more completely and successfully than has been done in England or Ireland, the great principles which are now considered to lie at the foundation of all prison discipline, and which have been exemplified so hopefully in Ireland, in Bavaria, and in Spain.

In my Annual Report I dwelt with some minuteness upon the great expense of our prison system; not because I regard economy as the chief object of such a system, however. The prevention of crime and the reformation of the criminal are the great objects of prison discipline, and any system which does not secure these, is costly at any price. But I expect to show, before I conclude, that we pay a high price without securing any adequate recompense.

I. THE ENGLISH CONVICT SYSTEM.

One feature of the English penal law—transportation—is still unknown to our jurisprudence—although, in our dealings with the southern rebels, it is not improbable that we may adopt it. It has been thoroughly tried, and is now almost wholly discarded by England, and instead of it, there has sprung up a class of punishments known as *Penal Servitude.*

(1.) *Penal Servitude and Ticket-of-Leave.*

This punishment was first introduced by name in the Act of Parliament of 1853 (16 & 17 Victoria, c. 99.) which substituted penal servitude for all sentences of transportation of less than fourteen years. In sentences above fourteen years, the Act gave the courts the discretionary power of sentencing either to transportation or penal servitude. The terms of punishment were prescribed, as follows: Instead of—

Transportation	*Penal Servitude*
For 7 years or less,	For 4 years.
Exceeding 7 years, and not exceeding 10 years,	Not less than 4 years, and not exceeding 6 years.
Exceeding 10 years, and not exceeding 15 years,	Not less than 6 years, and not exceeding 8 years.
Exceeding 15 years,	Not less than 6 years, and not exceeding 10 years.

In the case of life sentences only, there was no difference made.

Under this Act, power was given for the first time to the Home Office to grant licenses, or tickets-of-leave, to convicts of good conduct, to be at large, revocable at the pleasure of the crown. This system will be explained further on.

The effect of the Act of 1853, as respected convicts under sentence of transportation, and discharged from custody, was to substitute for the former practice of unconditional release with a free pardon, the grant of a ticket-of-leave, revocable for misconduct during the unexpired term of the sentence.

In 1856, a Committee of the House of Commons was appointed to inquire into the operation of the Act of 1853. That committee recommended that in every case, penal servitude should include—1st, a certain fixed period of imprisonment and hard labor; 2d, a further period which might be abridged by the convict's good conduct. The committee recommended that the sentences of penal servitude should be lengthened so as to be identical with the terms of transportation for which they were substituted.

Respecting the ticket-of-leave system, the committee, considering the short term during which it had been in operation, declined expressing any decided opinion; but recommended that the conditions indorsed upon the tickets should be more strictly enforced, and that every holder of a ticket-of-leave should be reported to the police of the town or district to which he was sent.

In 1857 an Act was passed to amend the Act of 1853. By this Act, sentences of transportation were prospectively abolished altogether, and penal servitude substituted. The provision that four years of penal servitude should be considered equivalent to seven years transportation, and so on, was repealed. A new sentence of three years penal servitude was added. Power was given to send convicts under sentence of penal servitude to any colony willing to receive them.

Under this Act a certain fixed term of the sentences is in all cases inflicted. But a remission of a certain term of the remaining portion is allowed for good conduct. The scale of remissions varies from one-sixth of the term in sentences of three years, to one-third in sentences of fifteen years and upwards. At first it was intended that the remission should in general, be unconditional, but this intention was subsequently departed from, and, as a rule, revocable licenses were, and continue to be, issued. Sentences for life are dealt with (as regards any remission,) according to the special circumstances of each case.

A Royal Commission appointed to inquire into the operation of the Acts of 1853 and 1857, made a Report on the 20th of June, 1863. From this Report and the evidence received by the Commissioners, valuable particulars of the working of the present system of Penal Servitude have been placed before the public, and I have made much use of it in these statements.

(2.) *Prisons and Prison Labor.*

In England, adult male convicts sentenced to Penal Servitude are first placed in separate confinement, usually for nine months, but occasionally for only eight months. The places of their detention are Millbank, Pentonville, and parts of Wakefield and Leicester Prisons. In these prisons the convicts are chiefly employed in tailoring, shoemaking, weaving, and mat-making. After six months good conduct, the prisoners receive a gratuity of 4*d*., 6*d*., or 8*d*., weekly, according to their industry, payable after discharge. At the end of the term of separate confinement, the convicts are removed to associated labor on public works. The ablebodied convicts are sent to Chatham or Portsmouth, (where there are large prisons with separate sleeping-cells for each,) and also to Portland or Gibraltar. The light-labor convicts are sent to Dartmoor, and the invalids to Woking. The convict establishment at Bermuda has lately been given up. The Hulk system has been altogether abolished; there has been no convict confined in the hulks since 1858.

The employment of the convicts at Chatham, where about 1,100 are ordinarily located, is mainly what is called "navvies' work," that is, excavating, and the rough work in building. Enormous docks are in course of formation at Chatham. At Portsmouth, the employment of the convicts is principally "dock-yard labor;" the majority are employed in scraping the bottoms of ships, or in loading and unloading colliers, or in cleaning chain-cables, scraping shot, etc. There was a party engaged in 1863 in levelling South-sea Common, and there were other parties employed at Haslar Hospital and in the Victualling Yard. At Portland, the work of the convicts consists principally in quarrying; a number of them are employed on the public fortifications and have exhibited workman-like skill as masons. They have also been most usefully employed on the great Breakwater. Generally speaking, the men take a pride in their work, if of a kind to bear evidence of their skill. Although working in associated labor (parties or gangs,) the convicts at Chatham and Portsmouth take their meals separately in their cells, as do the convicts in our prisons. A small number in each prison is employed as tailors, shoemakers, and cooks, and the carpentery, painting, etc., required in the prison are done by convicts. At Dartmoor, the prisoners are employed in reclaiming the land, draining and trenching; those unfit for that labour are employed in basket-making, mat-making, and picking oakum. At Woking there are only confirmed invalids; a number of whom are in a state of imbecility.

(3.) *Prison Discipline.*

Convicts employed on Public Works are subjected to three stages of discipline, in the lowest of which there are three Classes, and they are placed in those classes according to the report received of their conduct during their probation of separate confinement. Those placed in the second or third class are advanced to the next class, if exhibiting good conduct for three months. No convict is advanced beyond the lowest stage, unless he has first attained to the first class of that stage. If, having reached a higher stage, he is degraded for misconduct, he is reduced not only to the lowest stage, but also to a class in that stage below the first, until by good conduct he regains the first class, whence he may rise again to a higher stage by the exhibition of exemplary conduct.

The convict's general conduct is denoted by the class he is in, and if bad by a mark on his badge. A daily record is kept by the Warder under whom he works; his industry (or otherwise) being recorded by the same officer. The signs used are V. G. (very good;) G. (good;) and O. (ordinary.)

In the lowest stage, convicts are credited with the following gratuities: —

For Good Conduct: —

1st Class, per week,	6d.
2d " " "	4d.
3d " " "	0

For Industry: —

Very Industrious, (V. G.) per week,	9d.
Industrious, (G.) " "	6d.
Not Industrious, (O.) " "	0

After a convict has passed through the lowest stage, an advance to each of the subsequent stages entitles him to an additional weekly gratuity of 4d. for industry, and to certain other indulgences in diet, receiving letters, and visits from relations.

A convict may look for a remission of a portion of his sentence, if his record for industry and good conduct is satisfactory. The remissions are according to the following table: —

Remissions.

SENTENCE. Penal Servitude.	Proportion to be undergone.	Proportion that may be remitted for Good Conduct.
3 years,	Five-sixths, (2 years 6 months,)	One-sixth.
4 years,	Four-fifths, (3 years 3 months,)	One-fifth.
5 years,	Four-fifths, (4 years,)	One-fifth.
6 years,	Three-fourths, (4 years 6 months,)	One-fourth.
7 years,	Three-fourths, (5 years 3 months,)	One-fourth.
8 years,	Three-fourths, (6 years,)	One-fourth.
10 years,	Three-fourths, (7 years 6 months,)	One-fourth.
12 years,	Three-fourths, (9 years,)	One-fourth.
15 years and upwards,	Two-thirds,	One-third.

[*Commissioners' Report*, (1863,) *page* 130.]

A convict forfeits his claim to remission, in whole or in part, by misconduct; but by subsequent good conduct he may recover a portion of the time forfeited.

(4.) *The "Ticket-of-Leave."*

The Ticket-of-Leave is in each case granted by the Secretary of State for the Home Department. No convict's name is submitted unless he has been clear of all prison reports for misconduct for at least six months immediately preceding, and has also been industrious.

The following conditions are indorsed on the Ticket-of-Leave : —

"1. The License is liable to be revoked in case of misconduct.

"2. It may be revoked in the case of the holder of it being convicted of any new offence, unless the punishment for that offence extends beyond the term of his former sentence.

"But it is not necessary that the holder should be convicted of any new offence.

"If he associates with notoriously bad characters and leads an idle and dissolute life, with no visible means of obtaining an honest livelihood, he will be liable to be recommitted to prison under his original sentence.

"3. If his License is revoked, he may have to undergo the whole remaining portion of his original sentence."

No remission of sentence is allowed to a convict who has been reconvicted and sentenced to Penal Servitude while holding a Ticket-of-Leave.

The gratuity to which a convict may be entitled, when released, if not exceeding £5, is paid within ten days of his discharge; if it exceeds that sum, part is paid on discharge and the remainder by subsequent instalments, on the certificate of a magistrate, or the clergyman of the parish, or other competent and known authority, that the convict is earning his livelihood by honest means. In the metropolis, payment is made through the Police. When a convict is taken charge of by the Prisoners' Aid Society, the gratuity is paid to the Society, to be applied to his benefit.

(5.) *Convicts sent to Western Australia.*

These convicts are selected from those employed on the public works. The selection is made from those most physically able and most likely to be of service to the colony, and is generally regarded as a boon by the convicts themselves. In Western Australia a ticket-of-leave is obtained with more facility than in England, although each convict is debited with the number of marks which he must work off before he can receive a ticket. A ticket-holder is limited to a particular district, must not be out of his home after ten o'clock at night, and is subject to strict police supervision, with the liability of being brought back to punishment in the event of any irregularity.

(6.) *Juvenile and Female Convicts.*

Juvenile male convicts, under sixteen years of age, sentenced in England to Penal Servitude, undergo their sentences in Parkhurst Prison, in the Isle of Wight, where they are first kept in separate confinement, in the probationary ward, for four months, and are then employed in associated labor.

Female convicts, sentenced in England to Penal Servitude, are first sent to Millbank Prison, where they are kept about twelve months, a portion of that time in separate confinement. They are then sent to Brixton Prison, where the greater part of them remain until released with tickets-of-leave, or discharged at the expiration of their sentences. During their confinement at Millbank they are employed in making bags; and later, in needle-work and knitting, with the exception of those employed as cooks and laundresses. The well-conducted receive gratuities, according to a scale, for needle-work, laundry-work, etc.

At Brixton, the female prisoners are brought more into association, and have better food and pleasanter work. When they misconduct themselves, they are sent back to the penal class at Millbank. It was admitted in evidence before the Commissioners (2,247,) that nothing like a complete reformation, even of the best of the female convicts, takes place during their confinement at Brixton. A certain number, selected for their good conduct, are removed to the Fulham Refuge, which was opened in May, 1856. The number placed there is under 200, and they are engaged in several employments, principally washing; about one hundred are occupied daily in the laundry. They receive somewhat larger gratuities and have a better diet than at their previous places of confinement. Having passed through two stages of discipline at Millbank and three at Brixton, they pass through two more stages at Fulham, before obtaining a remission. Those not sent to Fulham obtain their remission at Brixton, when their conduct warrants them the privilege of a ticket-of-leave.

A fraction of the women, on leaving Fulham, find employment by the assistance of the Prisoners' Aid Society; also, some who are liberated direct from Brixton. Up to the close of 1862, the Society had assisted one hundred and eighty-eight females from Fulham, and one hundred and thirty-one from Brixton. Some of the females, when discharged, obtain admission into the Elizabeth Fry Refuge, whence they get into good situations in domestic service.

II. The Irish Convict System.

The Acts of 1853 and 1857 apply to Ireland as well as to England, but there are marked differences in the mode of administering the punishment of Penal Servitude in Ireland, as contrasted with England.

The chief value of the Report, Evidence, etc., before mentioned, is for the light thrown upon what is commonly known as "The Irish System." The features which distinguish this from the English system of Convict Discipline, were introduced by Sir Walter Crofton, who, in 1854, was appointed Chairman of the Directors of Convict Prisons in Ireland, he having for twelve months previous been one of the Commissioners to inquire into the state of the Irish Prisons. Sir Walter Crofton found a great want of classification in the Irish Prisons. With the ending of transportation (to Western Australia excepted,) the Irish authorities found thrown upon their hands a number of men who, if subjected to the English regulations merely, would have remained without hope of employment on their liberation, either under a license or by the expiration of their sentences. It was therefore determined to introduce certain improvements, including a more strict classification, and the Mark System. In his evidence, Sir W. Crofton disclaimed any credit for the last-named system, the introduction of which was owing to Captain Knight, who had been Governor of Portland and Portsmouth Prisons, and who, from his experience of the inefficacy of the classification in the English Prisons, was desirous of testing a new method of ascertaining the progress of the reformation of prisoners, which has been productive of the best results.

The original credit for the Mark System, however, is justly due to the late Captain Maconochie,* a practical philanthropist, to whom but scant justice, or positive injustice, was done in his day. After his long trials and difficulties, in connection with criminals, he did not lose his faith in human nature, and his belief that they might be raised by the adoption of a right system. " My experience leads me to say," he bore testimony to the Select Committee of 1856, " *that there is no man utterly incorrigible.* Treat him as a man, and not as a dog. You cannot recover a man except by doing justice to the manly qualities which he may have about him, and *giving him an interest in developing them.* I conceive that none are incorrigible where there is sanity ; there may be some proportion, but they are very small." But Captain Maconochie was actuated by no morbid sympathy with criminals. Until a man was really recovered, really fit for society, he would not restore him to it. " I would put temptation in his way, and *until he resisted that temptation he would not be fit for society.*" These are the fundamental principles of the Irish System, which, however, did not go into full operation until after the active services of Captain Maconochie had ended.

Sir Walter Crofton, in his evidence before the Commissioners, explained the objects he had in view in carrying out this system (Minutes of Evidence, page 253) :—

* See Appendix (A.)

"We had four points to bear in mind: — *First*, we were to discharge convicts, trusting that the community would meet us with regard to them, and must therefore train them so that the public would be induced to rely upon our tests, and give them employment. *Secondly*, we must protect the public during the time they employed them, by enforcing the conditions of the licenses, which enforcement was found to be a protection in the colonies, and appeared to be urgently required at home. *Thirdly*, and not the most easy task, to make the convicts fit for employment; and *Fourthly*, to induce voluntary emigration as far as possible.

In the first place, to induce employers to take rogues and thieves into their employment, was a problem beset with difficulty. It certainly could never have been accomplished by releasing them from the ordinary prison doors, or without exhibiting them in some more natural state than had been hitherto the case, and this brings me to the great and important difference, as I hold it to be, between the English and Irish systems. It was found necessary to supplement the ordinary system of discipline by an intermediate stage. It was quite evident that, to the public, a convict of good character in prison, and a good man, were two very distinct things. For example, a prisoner, in the absence of temptation, might go on very well and earn a good character, the greatest rogue often does; but if you place him where he would be under temptation, and where he would not have physical control over him, and let the public see that you so far believe in your own tests of training as to undertake the responsibility and risk of placing him in that position, it, accorded with common sense, as I think, that they would be more likely to employ him. It was an experiment, but it was based, in my mind, on reasonable grounds. The other great point of difference, was the institution of supervision after liberation; and here I at once acknowledge what has been adduced against us, that there must have been very weak faith on the part of the directors, in their own system, when they thought it necessary to supplement it by supervision after liberation. I acknowledge, and I am sure that my colleagues would do the same, that I have a weak faith in any mere prison system, and I think it far better, both for the public and the convict himself, to check his prison conduct and the prison system, by the infallible test of observation when he is at liberty."

(1.) *The Irish Prisons and Prison Labor.*

In Ireland, as in England, the punishment of Penal Servitude commences with separate confinement. The convict is sent to Mountjoy Prison, Dublin, his photograph is taken, and he is placed in separate confinement, similar to that at Pentonville Prison, London. He remains eight months, at the end of which term if his conduct has been good, he is placed at work in association with other convicts. But the slightest misconduct detains him another month, and it sometimes occurs that a convict is detained for twelve months before being placed in association. During the first four months of his separate confinement, meat is altogether excluded from his dietary. Formerly the convicts were put to work at, or to learn trades, as soon as they entered the prison; but under the new regulations the only work they are put to during the first three months is oakum-picking. This has a decidedly depressing effect upon them; so much so, that they regard more useful occupations as a most desirable change. After three months, those who have been shoemakers, or tailors, are put to work at their trades; others are employed in mending clothes and boot-closing, but are not taught any trade.

The prisoner is one hour every day at school, and the whole system of discipline is made the subject of School Lectures, by which the convict becomes thoroughly informed of the most important fact, that upon his own conduct depend the chances of a future remission of sentence, and, meanwhile, of certain ameliorations in his condition whilst still a prisoner.

At the expiration of the probationary term—eight months, or more, according to the convict's behavior—he is relieved from the irksomeness of separate confinement and sent to the Convict Prison at Spike Island, near the entrance to Cork Harbor. The greater number of prisoners are sent to Spike Island, but those of them who are tradesmen are sent to another wing of Mountjoy Prison, where the regulations are those of an associated prison. Here come into operation

(2.) *The Mark System, Gratuities, etc.* ⁓

Under which a convict behaving well obtains certain marks for good conduct under the three heads of Discipline, School, and Work. The work at Spike Island is principally quarrying, filling up holes, and paring down the surface of the rock to the sea to shape the fortification. As a rule, the men work willingly and well. The maximum number of marks each convict can obtain monthly is 9; that is,

3 for Discipline, for general regularity, and orderly demeanor.
3 for School; that is, not for attainment, but for industry in

school. A man learning his letters might get marks which another man of some education might not get.

3 for industry; that is, industry at work, not skill, which might have been previously acquired.

A man condemned to three years' Penal Servitude must show that he is in the first class, with 90 marks, before he can pass into the Intermediate Prison. On being taken from separate confinement, and placed in the associated labor Prisons, the convicts are placed in what is called the "third class," from which they may advance into the second and the first, and later into what is called the "A" or advanced class, which must be reached before the prisoner can pass to the Intermediate Prison. By attaining 18 marks, the convict may pass from the third [Associated Prisons] to the second class, in two months; by attaining 54 marks, he may pass from the second to the first class, in six months; and by obtaining 108 marks, he may pass from the first to the "A" or advanced class, in twelve months. When a convict has reached the advanced class, his conduct is noted as A1, A2, and so on. Any misconduct entails a reduction, or suspension, or loss of marks. On attaining to the "A" class, the convicts are removed to another part of the prison, and employed on special works.

Sir Walter Crofton testifies in the strongest language to the beneficial effects of the Mark System. [M. of E., p. 261.]

"I can record, from actual experience, that the marks are of the utmost value; they are the means of acting upon a man as an individual, and of realizing to him his own position, and his own means of progress. I know of no other way in which you can equally produce that effect upon him. I am quite satisfied that wherever the system of marks is tried it will succeed."

Sir W. Crofton added, that the system had been introduced into Wakefield (England) Prison, and among the convicts sent to Western Australia, where a similar system had been in operation for three or four years with the best effect.

No gratuities are allowed during the period of separate confinement. In the "Associated" Prison, there is placed to the convict's account 1d. a week in the third class, 2d. a week in the second class, 3d. and 4d. in the first class, (which is divided,) and from 7d. to 9d. a week in the " A " or advance class. The gratuities are about one-half what they are in England.

At Spike Island, the idlers and dangerous men are kept in classes distinct from the other prisoners. Both these sections are subsisted on low diet. The dangerous men, if once guilty of assaults on the officers, or other violence, are put in chains. These two classes are kept totally distinct from the other convicts, and otherwise punished, until they show by their conduct that they deserve to be put into the ordinary labor classes.

Under the system of classification above described, the Prison authorities at Spike Island, had (1863) been able to dispense with flogging for three years and a half.

The work done at the Associated Prison at Mountjoy is principally shoemaking and tailoring, with some carpentering, but only by a small class. The convicts work in association in large rooms, but sleep separately.

At Spike Island, the first, second and third classes work together, but sleep separately. The men of the " A'" class are employed in special works at Haulbowline. They work together, and take their meals together; they have schooling in the evening, and sleep in association.

(3.) *The Intermediate Prisons.*

One of the most important differences between the Irish and the English systems, is the existence, in connection with the former, of "Intermediate Prisons," to which such of the convicts as are considered fit for it, (according to the evidence, about 75 per cent. of the whole number,) are removed, after having undergone about four-sevenths of their sentences. These Intermediate Prisons are at Smithfield, in Dublin, and at Lusk, about fifteen miles from that city.

Smithfield (Intermediate) is an old prison, and the convicts sent there have been tradesmen. This was the first Intermediate Prison opened (November, 1855.) The gratuities credited to the convicts are based on a graduated scale, according to the work performed—a scale of price on each waistcoat, each pair of trousers, each pair of boots or shoes, etc.—but the maximum must not exceed 2s. 6d. a week each. The dietary is liberal. They are allowed to spend 6d. a week of their gratuity money. As a test of trustworthiness, each prisoner whose conduct continues good is allowed, under certain restrictions, to go into the streets of Dublin as messenger, to carry a mail bag, and to make purchases for the other prisoners within the amount above stated.

In the course of his evidence before the Commissioners, Sir W. Crofton read a statement which he had written in October, 1858, in defence of the system of Association, prefacing the reading of the paper by observing (Min. of Evidence, p. 268,)

"We discussed the matter seven and a half years ago, and Captain Whitty can state as distinctly as I can, that we have never had reason, for one moment, to regret having taken that course. If any person were to say to me now, 'Never mind the expense; it is better to have cells,' I should say, in principle, No; for my object is to show to the world that you can trust these men in association. I will read an answer that I gave with reference to this subject, because I consider it an important principle, both with regard to the association and the loss of the deterring effect. I have already given the reasons why these establishments were instituted, and I will now turn to the objection, as it has been set before the public very often, and give my reply to it. These observations were addressed to me publicly, and I replied to them—it is now four years and a half ago—and time and experience have only confirmed me in the opinion that I then expressed. 'The case on which objection to association is based, viz., the failure of the associated rooms at Portland, is perhaps the strongest argument to show the necessity of some further change in treating convicts before they are liberated. I believe the convicts so tried were all men of a high classification (first class;) if otherwise, the case is in no way to the point. If, then, notwithstanding the discipline of the early stages, the tone of the associated room of the first class prisoners was so bad as to induce the more exemplary to request removal to the cells, how is it possible to suppose that these first class men were well prepared for discharge, or that they could do well after liberation? This result is a further proof of the fallacy of an ordinary prison character, and is in accordance with the experience of the community. Directly the first class prisoner is placed in temptation, *i. e.*, in association, his real character comes forth. Hence the low appreciation of characters earned in prison; hence the difficulty experienced by convicts in getting employment through them. If discharged convicts could be guaranteed separate cells and absence from temptation, there would be no occasion to introduce a supplementary and a more natural stage before liberation takes place; but as there are no such appliances and exemptions, and as these men have been, and are for the future to be, discharged on the community at earlier periods of their sentence, in consequence of their good prison conduct, (note this with reference to the Act of 1857 especially,) we are bound, at whatever inconvenience, to test that conduct as far as it is practicable. In the case cited, it would have appeared a wiser course to have retained the more exemplary men in association, and to have removed the offending members to the cells, and thus to have raised the tone of the associated room; but with this I have no concern. The object of the association is, to test the character of men deemed in a more artificial state to be well conducted, and constant failures and consequent removals will no doubt take place from time to time. In due course, however, and under a proper system of training, the tone of the association will be what it is desirable to attain, and of such a nature as to improve those removed to it. I have no hesitation, after a very close and minute observation, during thirty-two months' experience, in affirming that this is and has been the case with several hundred prisoners, and that the conduct in these rooms will favorably compare with any association of laborers whatever.'"

Lusk. (Intermediate.) The convicts are encamped on the common, and are employed in draining and cultivating the land, and other out-door occupations. It is calculated that later the convicts may be employed in reclaiming other waste lands. They are not separated by any wall from the outer world, but free laborers do not come in contact with them. The diet is good, but the labor is severe. The prisoners take their meals, receive their schooling, and sleep in two large iron huts, each holding fifty men. The beds are put away in the daytime, and the place is well ventilated. There is placed half a crown (2s. 6d.) to the credit of each prisoner, if it is certified that he has done his work properly. Each is allowed to spend 6d. a week of his gratuity, and this is done as being to some extent a test of character. Some spend the 6d. a week one way, some another, and some not at all. Some spend that amount in bread, to add to their dietary; they are allowed to purchase tobacco to the extent of 6d., if they please, but not drink. Some, though they are very fond of smoking, exhibit great self-denial. The books they have they pay for by subscriptions out of their 6d. a week.

In the event of any misconduct either at Lusk or Smithfield, the convict is removed to Mountjoy, and placed in separate confinement. Since the system has been in operation there have been only two escapes from Lusk—both of the runaways were retaken—and but one from Smithfield, but this prisoner was not on external duty.

Some alarm was at first felt by the public in the neighborhood of Lusk, at the fact of a large number of convicts being placed in their vicinity, without being pent in by walls or other prison safeguards, but that alarm soon and completely subsided.

Lectures to the Prisoners.—Lectures are delivered to the prisoners at Smithfield and at Lusk by Mr. Organ, a man full of zeal, benevolence, and intelligence, and who has been for some years employed as lecturer to the Irish Intermediate Establishments. He discourses on subjects calculated to make the prisoners thinking beings; such as the properties of the air, water, plants, the ocean; also on temperance, the battles of life and how to fight them, etc. One object of the lectures is to inspire the men with a desire to emigrate to countries where there is a demand for labor, where the prisoner's antecedents will not be known, and where they will escape injurious contact with old associates in crime. Accordingly, among the prominent subjects of Mr. Organ's lectures, are Canada and her resources; Australia, past and present, etc., etc. The effect has been the voluntary emigration of a number of the best and most enterprising of the men who have listened to Mr. Organ's counsels.

(4.) *The Irish Ticket-of-Leave.*

This sketch may serve to indicate the Irish System of Penal Servitude up to the period when the convict, having passed through the several probationary and disciplinary stages already described, may be considered as having a fair claim to the privilege of being set at liberty under license, as provided by the Act of Parliament, the substance of which has been already recited.

The form of condition endorsed upon the ticket differs slightly from that now in use in England. The conditions are as follows:—

"1. The power of revoking or altering the license of a convict will most certainly be exercised in case of his misconduct.

"2. If, therefore, he wishes to retain the privilege, which by his good behavior under penal discipline he has obtained, he must prove by his subsequent conduct that he is really worthy of Her Majesty's clemency.

"3. To produce a forfeiture of the license it is by no means necessary that the holder should be convicted of any new offence. If he associates with notoriously bad characters, leads an idle and dissolute life, or has no visible means of obtaining an honest livelihood, etc., it will be assumed that he is about to relapse into crime, and he will be at once apprehended and recommitted to prison under his original sentence."

The Commissioners say that " great care appears to have been taken in Ireland to enforce these conditions." But here another leading difference in the Irish as contrasted with the English system, claims attention, that of

Police Supervision.—Discharged convicts returning to country districts are required to report themselves on their first arrival, at the constabulary stations of their respective districts, and subsequently on the first day of each month. The convicts at large in the Dublin district are not, however, required to report themselves, their supervision being undertaken by Mr. Organ, the lecturer, who reports to the Police only those with whose conduct he is not satisfied.

As already stated, the system of tickets-of-leave was first authorized by the Act of 1853, but then, and for some time subsequently, was applied only to convicts under sentences of transportation. The system was first applied to convicts sentenced to penal servitude under the Act of 1857, but did not come into operation until 1860. The law enacts that when it is determined to revoke a license, the magistrate is to issue his warrant for the apprehension of the convict, who, on identification, is to be committed to prison. But the Act makes no provision for any inquiry previous to the convict's arrest, nor does it afford him the opportunity to exculpate himself from any false accusation. Hence the disinclination of the Home Office to take action against the holder of a ticket-of-leave in England, on the mere *ex parte* statement of the Police that he is associating with bad characters or not leading an industrious life. The recommendation of the Committee of the House of Commons (1856) that the holder of a ticket-of-leave should be reported to the Police of the town or district to which he was sent, has not been carried into effect in England. At first the Secretary of State objected to grant licenses to convicts who had not a good prospect of obtaining employment, but it was found inexpedient to continue to act upon this rule.

(5.) *Employment of Discharged Prisoners.*

The last feature of the Irish System remains to be noticed. This is not a feature of the punishment of Penal Servitude, but supplementary thereto, the appropriate sequel to the means employed for the reformation of the convicts during the probationary, disciplinary, and intermediate stages of their punishment, previous to their obtaining tickets-of-leave.

Under the most favorable circumstances even men untainted by crime and of irreproachable character, often encounter difficulties in finding employment, more particularly if uninstructed in any trade. Men who have once suffered imprisonment, however penitent in spirit and morally reformed, find it almost impossible to obtain employment, and this is applicable to both countries. Thanks to the efforts of one enlightened and generous-hearted man, these difficulties have been overcome in a number of instances, and thereby a number of men have been saved from the frightful necessity of relapsing into crime. In addition to his labors as lecturer to the prisoners at Smithfield and Lusk, and the supervision of discharged convicts, so judiciously and praiseworthily exercised by Mr. Organ, that gentleman has made it part of his mission to endeavor to procure employment for the men placed under his surveillance. Describing his *modus operandi* he made the following interesting statement to the Commissioners: — (Minutes of Evidences, pages 372, 373; question 4,493.)

In answer to the question, " Will you explain to the Commission what steps you take in order to procure employment for those men on their discharge?" Mr. Organ replied as follows:—

"At the outset it was a labor of great difficulty. I commenced my duties in February, 1856; I drew out a map of the county of Dublin, dividing it into baronies, laying down upon this map the different post towns, also the mills, and factories, and farms, showing the names of the proprietors, the nature of their works, and so on. Having done this, I set out to see such and such employers. Sometimes I was scoffed at, and on more than one occasion the hall door was closed in my face. Still I persevered, and I was very well satisfied if, after going a distance of forty or fifty miles, I should meet with one employer who would give one of my Smithfield men a chance to work out his character once more. When I secured one, I visited both the employer and the employed, and I continue to do so down to the present time. The employer would ask me what control I had or the Government had over the men. I, of course, explained, but I will give a case in point. Some five years ago I went to a gentleman who was a very large employer, and I saw him. I explained to him my mission. I was a very long time in inducing him to give me a chance, but after many repeated visits I did succeed. He took one man. I visited that man once a fortnight, although he had removed from Dublin a distance of ten miles, and I visited the employer. That man succeeded in giving the employer satisfaction, and the employer afterwards applied for another, afterwards for another, and previous to my leaving Dublin this employer wrote the following letter, dated 21st February, 1863 : —

"' Dear Sir,—In reply to your letter, I beg leave to state that it was at your earnest solicitation I was induced to take convicts into my employment in the first instance. I have now had fully five years' experience of them, during which time they have given me universal satisfaction. I have one at present in my employment, in whose honesty I have such confidence that I have made him a sort of watchman, and he has for the last few days detected parties robbing me. Another saved enough to enable him to emigrate to Australia. A third, in shovelling up some manure, found a silver spoon, which he at once gave me. In conclusion I can only say that when you have an able-bodied man whom you can recommend, it will give me much pleasure to give him employment.'

"This employer was one whom I secured, I assure you, after a good deal of trouble, through the character and conduct of the first man he had employed."

Among the employers who have taken ticket-of-leave men on the recommendation of Mr. Organ, are several English and Scotch men. Mr. Organ testifies that he found the English more generously ready than the Irish to take the men on trial. The men with whom the ticket-of-leave holder is set to work, are of course not informed of the antecedents of their associate, for if they had that knowledge they certainly would refuse to work with him. This unhappy issue has occurred in two or three instances when the secret was not kept. A number of the reformed men emigrate, sometimes working their passage out, and sometimes paying their passage-money, at least in part, from the gratuities due to them for their prison labor; assistance being occasionally found for them by the exertions of Mr. Organ. That gentleman has received a number of letters from the emigrants, giving satisfactory assurances of their industry and prosperity, and their desire to assist their poor relatives with the means to emigrate.

Sir Walter Crofton in his evidence states that in consequence of the supervision that is exercised, employers now come forward in sufficient number to give most of the men who desire to do well a chance of obtaining an honest livelihood. Those failing to obtain immediate employment, but resolutely resolved to live by honest work, can usually obtain the means to emigrate. Of nine hundred and thirty license holders liberated from the Intermediate Prisons, three hundred and ninety-seven have emigrated. Mr Organ stated that not more than five per cent. of those discharged from the Intemediate Prisons have relapsed.

(6.) *Police Supervision.*

As the obtaining of employment for the convicts discharged with tickets-of-leave is clearly dependent upon the supervision maintained over them, some further account of Mr. Organ's method may here be given from the Minutes of Evidence. (Pages 374, 375.)

"I divide my visitation reports into three parts, one showing the number under the old transportation Act; the next showing the number unconditionally discharged, over whom the Government have no control; and the next relates to the Penal Servitude Act of 1857 that gave those short sentences.

"Here is a case, for instance, of a man who was sentenced for ten years for receiving stolen goods, and having under his pillow a blunderbuss; his former character is this:—

"A terror to the neighborhood in which he resides; his residence is about four miles from Dublin; his employer is Mr. So and So; he has remained with his employer since the 9th of April, 1856; he has been from that hour under my supervision; and my last remark was this: 'A man of sober and settled habits, writes Mr. So and So, for the last seven years, wife sober and industrious, has a pig and fowl. His period of license expired on the 3d of January, 1862; he was from 1856 to

1862 on license; but with that kind of connection that exists between me and the discharged convicts we are not ashamed to know one another, provided no one sees us. [Mr. Organ added that he found that man his employment.] " There is another transported man here; he was five years under my supervision. * * * This man was discharged in 1857, and he is earning eight shillings and sixpence per week; he has been with the same employer since he was discharged. That employer, you must understand, first took the ticket-of-leave men over whom the Government had a control, and had in his employ seven of them at a time; they earned good characters for themselves; but I sent this man over whom there was no control, and yet he followed in the wake of the others, and remained there; he is working now for eight shillings and sixpence a week, but he is not an able-bodied man or fit for strong work; he walks seven miles in on Saturday evening to share that eight shillings and sixpence with a wife and child; this is an unconditionally discharged man. Now I will refer to the men under the Act of 1857. The first man on my list was discharged on the 6th of February, 1861; felony was his last crime; he had been thirteen times convicted before, and had been known as a thief since 1845; his name and residence are here put down, and his employment, as before he was last sentenced to four years; the observation is this: Keeping from crime, contrary to the opinion of many who knew him before.' [Mr. Organ added that he had now been discharged two years and more, and was in employment.] * * *

" Referring to the connection between the Police and myself, when I find a man that is not going on according to my liking, and he has something suspicious about him, I go to the director, and I either bring the man up, if within reach, or tell him about him. I say, 'I do not like the way in which this man is going on;' he may have too smooth an appear- for a hard-working man, or he may be lounging about, or I might find him in his home when he should be out working, or out when he should be in; then the director takes a note of that; at the same time if it happens that my suspicions are aroused at night, or when the director is not in the office, and the case is an urgent one, I do not wait for the director to come the following morning, but I go straight into the detective office at the castle-yard; I there tell the officiating inspector my doubts, and he, as a matter of course, has a close eye upon that man. Then in cases of suspicion I inform the detective authorities; they know that it is their interest and my interest to work hand-in-hand; and I point out to them sometimes, when I have my documents convenient, the last observation I have made upon the man."

In answer to a question, Mr. Organ explained the nature of his intercourse with the detective police; in addition to the above accounts, reading the following letter: — (Minutes of Evidence, page 373.)

13, RICHMOND FAIRVIEW, Co. DUBLIN,
January 10, 1863.

SIR,—In reply to your inquiry into my opinion of the working of the ticket-of-leave system in Ireland, I beg to submit the following statement of my practical experience, day and night, of the Smithfield men discharged on license, and otherwise, and working and residing in the city and county of Dublin. It is perhaps necessary that I should state that I have been a detective police officer for eleven years, and therefore had an opportunity of making myself acquainted with the working of the new and old system of convict management in Ireland; my experience of the old system was of a most painful character, for the criminals came out of the prison worse in fact than they entered, whereas on the other hand I have known very bad characters when discharged from your intermediate prisons to engage in steady labor, earning their bread and absorbed amongst the honest members of the working community. It must have been only by perseverance that any Irish employer of respectable position could be induced to take into his work men who had been habitual thieves and burglars; for the aversion of all men of respectability in Ireland to employ convicts is very great. By this constant intercourse with the directors and yourself, I have on very many occasions been enabled to prevent the commission of additional crime by visiting the abodes of the persons we had reason to believe intended doing wrong. We have never known a man discharged, and under your supervision, to be convicted of any act bordering upon violence on the person. I think the fact of a numerous and influential class of employers who have many of your discharged convicts in their establishments is a proof of the great good which has resulted from the of the Irish convict system. I am prepared and willing, at any time, to give information in detail wherever circumstances may require me to do so. I remain, &c., TIMOTHY MURPHY,
Late Acting Inspector Detective Department, Dublin Metropolitan Police.
To JAMES P. ORGAN, Esq., &c., &c.

Sir Walter Crofton, in his evidence in relation to this subject, stated that the plan of the Dublin supervision was that the lecturer should visit every man out on ticket-of-leave, officially, and bring in a return every fortnight, showing the employer's name, the standard of wages, and the conduct of the men. This return was filed, and the information was afterwards checked by a detective inspector of police. If Mr. Organ found that there was any obstruction to his obtaining from the convict full information, the latter was at once handed over to the observations of the police. The slightest infringement of a license leads to its revocation.

Supervision in the Country.—Finding that some of the discharged men went into the country, the necessity was seen of having police supervision there. The said supervision is carried on thus: A notification is made to the inspector-general of the constabulary when a man is liberated, stating to what district he is going. Arrived in the district, the man reports himself to the head of the police of that district, states what he is going to do, where he is going to be employed, etc. He has to report himself once a month. If he removes, his registration is transferred to the new district he proposes to live in. If he infringes the conditions of his license the constabulary report him, and his license is at once revoked. There is no undue interference or espionage by the police. The public generally are satisfied with the system of supervision, and regard it as a necessary and valuable protection. The supervision in the country, though not so efficient as in Dublin, is ample, and sufficiently protective of the public welfare. There was more espionage in Ireland before the systematic supervision of convicts than there has been since. From the fact of there being a police supervision in the country, and an efficient supervision in Dublin, a much more accurate means of knowing what the convicts are really doing can be obtained, than in England, not only as to ticket-of-leave men, but also as to the class of discharged convicts, numbering nearly 500 in 1863.[*]

[*] The work undertaken by Mr. Organ in finding employment for discharged prisoners in Ireland, is undertaken in England by the Prisoners' Aid Society, established within the last seven years in London. Of 12,691 prisoners discharged, 2,800 had been assisted by the society, of whom 280 males had emigrated. As before stated, when a convict is taken charge of by this society, the gratuity due to him for prison labor is paid to the society to be applied for his benefit. [The preceding figures are taken from the evidence of Sir J. Jebb, (Minutes, page 43,) but in the evidence of W. B. Ranken, (Minutes, pages

(7) *Female Convicts and Female Refuges.*

The female convicts are first sent to Mountjoy Prison. All classes are there kept four months in strict separation in what is called the probationary stage. They are moved into the third class upon the same principle as the men, for two months. If a woman conducts herself well in the third class, she is removed into the second, where she remains for six months. If she obtains the necessary number of marks, she attains to the first class, and in the same way subsequently to the advanced class. While in the third class, a woman is kept in her cell, the same as if on probation, receiving merely 1d. a week gratuity. Removed to the second class, her cell door remains open during half the day. In the first class, those sleeping separately work in association in a room. In the advanced class, they are put together in a room, and kept by themselves in another part of the building, and employed in the laundry and at other special occupations. There is also a refuge class, and those in that class are kept by themselves. The system of marks, and the opportunity for a female convict to work herself out of one class into another, is as far as can be similar to that pursued in the case of the men, with this difference, that the men are kept nine months in separate confinement, and the women only four. But when they obtain their marks for each stage, they are advanced in a similar manner. Yet in a general way the women are kept more strictly as to their separation than are the men. In the second and third classes they do not associate in work as the men do. No female is discharged on license unless some guarantee is given that there is a home for her to go to.

There are two Refuges in Ireland, established in 1856. It was found impossible to get women into domestic service or other employment if it was known that they came directly from

432, 433,) it is stated that the society has assisted 3,142 cases, (males and females,) in six years, and that the number assisted to emigrate in the course of that time amounted to 868, principally males.] The evidence respecting the operations of this society is scanty, but there is every reason for doubting that the system followed is as productive of good results as that followed by Mr. Organ, owing to the want of the supervision exercised in Ireland. In the cases of those who emigrate the results may be as satisfactory, as in the instances of the emigrants from Ireland, but there is nothing in the Minutes of Evidence on this subject.

a prison. Hence the establishment of the Refuges. One of these is at Golden Bridge, near Dublin, for Roman Catholics; the other in Heytesbury Street, in that city, for Protestants, managed by a committee of ladies. Female convicts under punishment for grave offences, and invalids suffering under serious maladies, are not sent to the Refuges. The efforts of the ladies at the head of these establishments have been very successful in obtaining employment for the women. The Refuges are a valuable adjunct to the Penal Servitude System. It should be stated that the Golden Bridge Refuge is superintended by Sisters of Charity.

Mention has already been made of the Fulham Refuge for female convicts in England. Sir Joshua Jebb, in his Evidence before the Commissioners, (Minutes, p. 56,) gives preference to the Fulham Refuge over the Irish Refuges.

III. THE PARLIAMENTARY COMMISSION OF 1863.

In their Report the Commissioners proceeded to consider the results of the system of punishment (in England and Ireland) above described, and in what respects it might be susceptible of improvement. According to their view, penal servitude was not sufficiently dreaded by the criminal classes, and this they attributed mainly to the shortness of the punishment inflicted upon many of the convicts; second, to the defects in the prison discipline; third, to the want of proper supervision of convicts released on tickets-of-leave; fourth, to the absence of any efficient method in detecting recommitted offenders.

The Commissioners denounced the evil of short sentences of punishment, being sustained in this by the evidence recorded in the Minutes. It will be sufficient to name the two most prominent authorities, viz., Sir Joshua Jebb, and Sir Walter Crofton, as having concurred with the Commissioners in condemning the above-named evil. Sir J. Jebb expressed the opinion that the sentence of three years' penal servitude was a mistake, being insufficient to operate as a deterrent. He added that, in his judgment, five years ought to be the minimum sentence. Sir W. Crofton concurred in the above estimate of the inefficiency of the three years' sentences. In his opinion, no old offender should be sentenced to less than seven years' penal servitude.

The Commissioners were strongly of opinion that the system of allowing convicts to earn a remission of a part of their punishment by industry, should be maintained ; they considered the regulations relating to remissions in force under the English system to be needlessly complicated and otherwise objectionable ; they deemed the Irish rules more commendable, but added, " that these rules have the fault of not providing that each day's greater or less degree of industry on the part of a convict, should be so recorded as to have an influence on the period of his discharge." The Commissioners objected to the credit given for general good conduct, meaning, in a prison, abstaining from misconduct. They also objected to the Irish practice of giving marks for diligence in school.

The Commissioners preferred the mark system applied to the convicts in Western Australia, " where the convicts are allowed to earn a number of marks depending upon their industry, with the right of obtaining tickets-of-leave when their total earnings reach an amount calculated according to the length of their sentence. No credit is given them for good conduct, but they are liable to forfeit the marks they have earned, by fines imposed upon them for bad conduct.".

The Commissioners expressed their approval of the supervision of license-holders, who, they suggested, should be placed under the supervision of an officer of the convict department, aided by proper assistants to fulfil the duties performed in Dublin by Mr. Organ, the police not to interfere in the supervision unless when required by the proper officers. They made further suggestions relative to the license-holders.

Recognizing the difficulties discharged convicts have to meet with in seeking employment, the Commissioners were of opinion that as many convicts as possible should be sent to Western Australia. This, for reasons already assigned, is not likely to be acted upon, or, if acted upon, only for comparatively a short time.

The Commissioners considered it advisable that the minimum sentences of penal servitude should be for seven years, with the privilege granted to the convict of earning a reduction of that term, the remission to be regulated by allowing him one day's reduction for a certain number of marks.

The Commissioners strongly urged the continuance of the probationary term of nine months' separate confinement, and its rigid enforcement; at the same time expressing approval of the Irish treatment of prisoners undergoing separate confinement.

They recommended a more distinct classification of the English prisoners employed in public works; also, an increase in the severity of corporal punishment in some cases. Objecting to day-schooling, they recommended night-schooling, as in Ireland. They approved of convicts being employed on works, the utility of which would be most likely to excite them to greater industry and the acquisition of mechanical skill, besides being of much greater advantage to the public. The Commissioners favored the idea of setting the convicts to task-work, notwithstanding that most of the evidence they had heard was opposed to its practicability. They objected to the English system of gratuities, which they suggested should be allowed only after the convicts had passed through a considerable portion of their punishment. The privilege allowed to Irish convicts, in an advanced stage, of spending a weekly portion of their gratuities, the Commissioners approved, as an additional incentive to good conduct.

In the case of female convicts, the Commissioners recommended a larger remission of sentence, and some improvements in the treatment of refractory women. They added : " We consider that the case of discharged female convicts, is one that recommends itself peculiarly to the consideration of the benevolent; and we believe that charitable and religious societies are the only means whereby the dangers which always await a female convict on her discharge from prison, can be lessened."

The Commissioners concluded their report with a récapitulation of the most important of their recommendations, as follows (Report, p. 72) :—

" 1. That sentences of penal servitude should not, in future, be passed for shorter terms than seven years.

" 2. That the principle, already recognized by the law, of subjecting re-convicted criminals to severer punishment, should be more fully acted on.

" 3. That convicts sentenced to penal servitude should be subjected, in the first place, to nine months' separate imprisonment, and then to labor on public works for the remainder of the term for which they are sentenced, but with the power of earning, by industry and good conduct, an abridgment of this part of their punishment.

"4. That all male convicts, who are not disqualified for removal to a colony, should be sent to Western Australia during the latter part of their punishment.

"5. That those who may be unfit to go there, but may earn an abridgment of their punishment, and who may consequently be discharged at home, under license, should be placed under strict supervision till the expiration of the terms for which they were sentenced, and that the necessary powers should be given by law for rendering this supervision effectual."

Three of the Commissioners objected to the Recommendations of the majority. Mr. J. W. Henley objected to the Ticket-of-Leave System, as unsuited to the country, and injurious to the convict and to society. The Lord Chief Justice, Sir A. E. Cockburn, in an elaborate memorandum, dissented from the Report generally, and specially to the recommendations touching the lengthening of sentences, and the placing of license-holders under supervision, considering the alleged success of the latter in Ireland as due to exceptional circumstances not likely to exist in England. He also objected to any remission of punishment, excepting in a penal colony (colonial penal establishment.) As regards convicts detained at home, he considered punishment should be made as rigorous as consistent with health of body and mind. Being rendered rigorous, it should not be prolonged beyond what is necessary to deter from crime; but that the sentence of the judge, once pronounced, the punishment should be suffered for the full and entire period of the sentence. Hugh C. E. Childers, though signing the Report, objected to the recommendations relative to transportation, as costly to the country and odious to the colonies, and only at best affording a brief delay in the solution of a question daily becoming more difficult.

IV. THE TWO SYSTEMS OF ENGLAND AND IRELAND COMPARED.

Originally, the two systems of convict discipline were nearly identical, at least in theory:—

In Ireland, the system consists of, 1st, Separate Confinement; 2d, Associated Imprisonment, mainly upon public works; 3d, Imprisonment with an amount of freedom bordering on liberty in the Intermediate Prisons; 4th, Conditional Liberty under Police Supervision.

In *England*, the system, as originally designed, consisted of, 1st, Separate Confinement; 2d, Labor in Association on public works, but without the association in sleeping, etc., of the Irish System; 3d, Imprisonment with a considerable amount of liberty *in the Colonies;* 4th, Conditional Liberty under Police Supervision *in the Colonies*.

But from the time when Transportation ceased, (excepting the comparatively few convicts sent to Western Australia,) the third and fourth stages of the above were judged inexpedient as regards England. Conditional remissions were allowed for good conduct and industry, as already explained, but it was considered impracticable or impolitic to bring the ticket-of-leave holders under supervision.

In truth, the resemblance between the two systems was at any time more seeming than real, and can hardly be said to have extended beyond the first stage. In the second stage, although under both systems the majority of the convicts are employed on public works, in England that stage is protracted to the moment of liberation, whether by expiration of sentence or by a license of conditional remission. In Ireland that stage is abridged to allow time for a final probation in the Intermediate Prison. In England, the prisoner, on his release, though stringent conditions are indorsed on his paper, is unwatched and unrestrained; in Ireland, he is under the constant supervision of the police until the expiration of the term of his original sentence and the consequent termination of his license, when he becomes absolutely free.

Captain Whitty, the successor of Sir W. Crofton in the direction of the Irish System, in his evidence before the Commissioners, thus succinctly summed up the points in which the Irish System differs from the English:—

1st, The greater stringency in the first period of the sentence; 2d, A more minute plan of classification on the public works as the second stage; 3d, A lower scale of gratuity in the earlier stages in the Irish prisons, the higher rates being reserved for the later and superior classes; 4th, The Intermediate Prisons, which are a special means of mental improvement, and of preparing the prisoners for the transition from confinement to liberty, and also of testing their preparation; 5th, A more rigid enforcement of the conditions on which the prisoners are set at large on license; 6th, A process of tracing back and placing before the judges the cases of habitual offenders.

The chief distinctive features of the Irish, as contrasted with the English System, are, then,

(1.) Intermediate Prisons;
(2.) Police Supervision.

(1.) *Intermediate Prisons.*—The time that a prisoner is kept in an intermediate prison depends upon the length of his sentence. A man sentenced to seven years' penal servitude would be fifteen months in the intermediate prison; under ten years' sentence he would be six years in an ordinary prison, and if he conducted himself properly, a year and a half in an intermediate prison. If his conduct continued satisfactory during that time, he would at the end of that period be liberated on ticket-of-leave. The nature of the discipline in the intermediate prisons has been already described, as also that of the prisoners working, sleeping, etc., in Association. But it may not be superfluous to copy a paragraph from a paper read by Sir W. Crofton at the meeting of the Social Science Association, held in London in 1862, (Volume of *Transactions*, pp. 375, 376) :—

"We had to conciliate public opinion, not by words, but by deeds. We had to demonstrate that our prison training had so improved the convict that he might be offered employment without alarm. We did not wish to have to add — but you must keep him in a cage and hire a man to look after him, or he will assuredly relapse. We had also to show to the convicts themselves that our faith in their amendment was not a mere sham — that their exertions should receive our confidence. I cannot exaggerate the advantage of this settled conviction in the mind of the convict. We knew that in the world the convict would have to be employed and located as other ordinary laborers, and I would ask, if we felt that the worst consequences would ensue through placing these men together before liberation, how could we — more than this, how dare we — find fault with the public for not offering them employment? The convict's training must be in accordance with public opinion, or his absorption into the community will be impossible. He will remain forever one of a distinct class, to be shunned, but not to be assisted. The Portland failure was not to the point, for on the face of the statement it was not conducted systematically — the well and ill-conducted were located together. The tone of that associated room indicated that previous training had neither made the inmates fit for it nor for liberty. But what has been the result of six years' experience of this system, which has been likened to that of the hulks — of this dangerous, retrograde, and demoralizing system? That not one convict has given cause for offence on immoral grounds."

(2.) *Police Supervision.*—It is not surprising that the question of police supervision should have been a bone of contention between very able and philanthropic men embracing the most opposite views, from conscientious motives. The term Police Supervision is altogether new to the vocabulary of English law and its administrators. When the thing itself had to be described, it was always, until recently, designated by the French word *surveillance*, a system held to be totally at variance with the spirit and practice of British institutions. In France, the police *surveillance* over those who have been convicted of heinous offences, and subsequently set at liberty by the expiration of their sentences or otherwise, is by virtue of a law which specially directs it to be part of their sentence. Numerous memoirs, and other publications, have recounted the odious character of the tyranny in many cases exercised by the French police over the wretched beings, not always impenitent ruffians, subjected to their supervision. These stories, some the creations of romance-writers merely, others unquestionably too true, have tended to strengthen the English dislike of any such system. Eminent authorities have expressed their profound conviction that police supervision would be fatal to any chance of procuring employment, which the liberated convict might otherwise hope to obtain. For example —

Questioned whether placing the ticket-of-leave holders under the *surveillance* of the police would assist them in procuring employment, Sir J. Jebb answered emphatically : " Quite the reverse." Sir R. Mayne testified to the same effect, and stated that the Prisoners' Aid Society was quite opposed to any such interference. This was confirmed by W. B. Rankin, Secretary to the Society, who stated that it was designed to have the men committed to the Society's aid placed under the supervision of the Society's agents only, without the police interfering, except on the requisition of the Association. Lord Chief Justice Cockburn, in his Memorandum, (see Appendix to the Commissioners' Report,) objects to any supervision by the police or other officers appointed for the purpose, on the ground " that such supervision would be fatal to the convict's chance of obtaining employment. Police supervision would be incompatible with the concealment of the man's antecedents, while, in the great majority of instances, the well-doing of a convict must depend on his secret being kept. Few masters would employ a man who is known to be a convicted felon, and an equal obstacle would be found in the disinclination of other laborers to be associated with one thus degraded. * * * The system of *surveillance* so largely tried on the Continent, has been found to work very ill. In France, it has lately been discontinued to a great extent."

To these objections the working of the Irish system and its practical results are brought forward by its supporters as a sufficient reply.

(3.) *Results of the Two Systems.*

(a.) *England.*—From a paper read by Sir Joshua Jebb, at the meeting of the Social Science Association, held in London, in 1862, (Volume of *Transactions*, pp. 363, 364,) the following is extracted :—

"The results of the discipline, so far as relapses are concerned, are given in detailed returns in my reports, from which it appears that of 10,507 male convicts released on license in the $8\frac{1}{4}$ years between October, 1853, and December, 1861, 8 per cent. only have had their license revoked, and 10.7 per cent. have been again sentenced to penal servitude. Of these 13.6 per cent. have been convicted of light offences and misdemeanors, and 5.1 per cent. only of more serious crimes. A strong proof of the effect of the discipline is afforded by the success of the Prisoners' Aid Society. Out of 189 cases from Millbank prison, and 574 from Chatham prison, entertained by that society, only a single license has been revoked. * * *

"In the year 1853, there were issued 335 licenses. One was revoked in that year, 7 in 1854, 3 in 1855, 2 in 1856, 2 in 1857, making 15 in all, or 4.5 per cent. in $7\frac{1}{2}$ years to the date of the return."

Two years ago, (that is, in 1862,) Mr. Recorder Hill said, " From observation and inquiry, continued for many years, I have arrived at the conclusion that the number of English relapses must exceed 50 per cent."

(b.) *Ireland.*—From a paper read by Sir Walter Crofton at the above-mentioned meeting, the following is extracted: (Volume of *Transactions,* pp. 373, 374, 377.)

"I now come to the practical results of this Act of 1857, as evinced in the Irish Convict Prisons, which, it must be remembered, also contain convicts sentenced under former statutes. The number released under this Act up to the 1st of January, 1862, has been 415. 269 of this number were male convicts, and only 41 of them failed, through want of the required marks, to reach the intermediate prisons.

"On coming to the most real and satisfactory test of amendment, —'liberty,'—we find that since the commencement of the discharges under this Act in 1859, up to January, 1862, they amounted to 415. Only 27 of these have returned to either convict or county prisons for criminal offences. Considering the appliances in force for bringing old offenders to the knowledge of the authorities in Ireland, this is a satisfactory result. But it would have been still more so, had sufficient time been allowed, by the length of sentences passed on 'Habitual Criminals,' to both increase the period of prison training and of conditional liberation.

"Our experience under this Act is therefore :—

"1st. That a very large proportion of the convicts make strenuous efforts to reach the intermediate prisons, and attain them.

"2dly. That they are placed in this more natural position at which they have arrived sooner or later, according to the attainment of their marks, with extremely good results, both to themselves and the public.

"3dly. That they show by their subsequent conduct that they value the lessons which they have learned, and are making application of them in the fields of temptation."

*   *   *   *   *

"We have, for many years past, been introducing measures calculated to reduce our criminal population. The reformatory schools hold under detention nearly 4,000 between the ages of sixteen and twenty-oné, who are, at all events for the time, withdrawn from criminal pursuits. We have also the large number liberated, and we hope amended, by means of the training received in these establishments. It may be reasonably assumed that in former days these juveniles and adults—for very many of them have long since become adults—would have helped to fill both Parkhurst and the other convict prisons."

The system of *Association*, carried to the length it is in Ireland, has been warmly contested, but has received the approving sanction of a considerable number of responsible persons. Sir Walter Crofton's able defence of this system before the Commissioners, has been already cited. It will not be out of place to make the following additional extract from a paper read by that gentleman at the Social Science Congress, 1863, (Volume of *Transactions*, p. 406) :—

"In Ireland, it has been found that the exhibition of convict labor in a state of comparative freedom from restraint, tends to give confidence to employers, and conduces to this end. Common sense, I think, points to the same result in whatever country it is tried. As we shall be obliged to liberate a large number of convicts at home, I feel assured that some such course as this must sooner or later be adopted in England, in order to promote the employment of the well-intentioned. I am satisfied that hutting convicts, and utilizing their labor over the country in harbors of refuge and fortifications, will be the means of improving the convicts, assisting their employment, and prove a great economy to the public. If it is considered to be too hazardous to try the plan exactly in the same form as in Ireland, let the male convicts pass the early period of their licenses to be at large in these huts. If they don't conduct themselves well in this their first state of liberty, let them be returned to prison, instead of having their licenses extended."

In connection with this subject, there should be noticed a suggestion by Mr. C. P. Measor, late Deputy-Governor of Chatham Convict Prison, in a paper on "The Reformatory Principle in Criminal Punishment," (Volume of *Transactions*, 1863, p. 465) :—

"He held that labor should take its place among the higher appliances of reformation, rather than among the primary elements of punishment. To render it anything but a boon, and a means of attaining the various grades of privilege, was to sacrifice its power of strengthening self-respect. As the basis of reformatory discipline, labor became the nucleus of many virtues, and in it was to be found the true leverage by which to raise the criminal. Upon this principle, restraint for the good of society became its punishment, and labor the prisoner's means for its mitigation. The directors of the Irish Convict Prisons had, he thought, put labor in its proper place, by compelling the prisoner to seek it as a boon, and relief from the monotony of solitude. He suggested that convicts should be allowed to employ their spare hours in working for a fund for the relief of those dependent upon them, and that those who had no relations dependent upon them might be allowed to contribute. He thought this an instance in which the reformatory principle had not been extended so far as it ought. There was full scope here for assigning value to works of supererogation, for the man's own sake, to acts of good feeling towards others, and to the claims of those naturally dependent upon him."

In the year 1861, the Annual Congress of the Social Science Association was held in Dublin, when an array of judges, legislators, magistrates, managers of reformatory schools, governors of gaols, and others, visited the prisons conducted under the regulations of the Irish System. They also tested the results by visiting and questioning employers who had taken discharged convicts into their service; and Lord Brougham, in his address at the opening of the meeting the following year in London, referring to the above investigation, said, (Volume of *Transactions*, 1862, p. 10):—

"In many instances conclusive proof was given of the permanent good effects wrought by the training which the prisoners had received. The masters who already employed convicts. went themselves to the prisons to engage other prisoners who were on the eve of discharge, lest they should be too late by the time the discharge was completed. The conclusion at which we arrived, so far as I know, was unanimous. It placed the Irish Convict System far above all others which had been subjected to the test of experience, for its success in accomplishing the great object of its institution—the reformation of the criminal; and I may add, that what we witnessed in Ireland has created an ardent desire throughout England that we may as soon as possible enjoy the same advantages at home."

At a meeting of the Council of the Association, held on the 17th of February, 1863, at Burlington House, London, the following Resolutions were unanimously adopted:—

"1. That the failure of the present system of convict discipline in England is chiefly due to the short sentences frequently passed on habitual criminals, the want of an efficient probationary stage for convicts under sentence, and of police supervision over discharged prisoners.

"2. That these defects would be remedied by adopting and carrying out the principles of the convict system which has been so successfully administered in Ireland."

(4.) *Comparative Expense of the Two Systems.*
"Under the English System," said the Rev. W. L. Clay, before the Social Science Congress in 1862, "a convict costs rather more than £35; under the Irish System, rather less than £25, a year." This difference, expressed in our currency, in ordinary times, would be as $175 (or $3.36 per week,) is to $125 ($2.40 per week;) both sums being considerably higher than the cost at our State Prison, even for the past year ($1.38 per week.) Both are lower, however, than the cost of supporting prisoners in our county prisons, which has averaged for the year ending October 1, 1864, $3.43 per week. It is charged, however, by those who object to the Irish System, that it cost almost as much as the English System, or upwards of £32 for each convict in 1862. The official returns published in the Report of the Parliamentary Commissioners, state the expenses in Ireland to have been as follows:—

In 1859–'60, for 1,672 prisoners, each £16.87, say $84.
In 1860–'61, for 1,521 prisoners, each £17.2, say $85.
In 1861–'62, for 1,354 prisoners, each £18.59, say $92.
In 1862–'63, for 1,477 prisoners, each £10.15, say $50 (9 months.)

These expenses are divided among four prisons, giving to each an average of between 350 and 400 prisoners for the four years, or about the average number at Charlestown for the last year; the weekly cost, too, is for 1862–'63, only about $1.45 a week, or a trifle more than the expense at Charlestown for the last year. But it is no doubt true that the cost of convict prisons, both in England and Ireland, is greater than that of American Penitentiaries, if we except the Prison at Philadelphia, conducted on the *Separate*, or *Solitary* system.* It is charged by a well-informed Englishman, already quoted, (W. L. Clay,) that our Penitentiaries "had their origin more in

---

* I use these terms (contrary to their former application,) as signifying the same kind of imprisonment, for the term *Solitary* has been improperly applied to the *Congregate* system.

dollar-worship, than in philanthropy." From this sweeping, but not wholly unjust accusation, he exempts Massachusetts. "In Connecticut, Massachusetts and Pennsylvania alone," he says, "was the salvation of felons more valued than the profits of their labor."

There is good reason to believe that the Irish System, if tried here, would be found far less costly than in Ireland, since the profits of labor would be much greater, in proportion to the cost of support. A similar advantage would exist here, in the greater ease of finding occupation for the discharged prisoners, and those on Ticket-of-Leave.

(5.) *Recent Legislation.*

Thus far the English System of Penal Servitude and Convict Discipline as revealed by the Report of the Commissioners of 1863, has been spoken of in the present tense, and correctly, for that system is probably still in force. But a great change has been provided for by recent legislation, which change will shortly be seen in operation. The evidence given by the Royal Commissioners, the Report of the Commission, the inquiry promoted by the Social Science Association, and the zealous labors of Mr. Recorder Hill, and other able and energetic reformers have produced legislative results calculated to bring the English System more into accord with that which (according to evidence,) has been so fruitful of good in Ireland.

In the late session of the Parliament of Great Britain, (1864,) an Act was passed to amend preceding Acts relating to Penal Servitude and Convict Discipline.

The following, among other changes, are enacted by the new law:—

1. The *minimum* of Penal Servitude is raised from three to five years, to allow sufficient time for the various stages of probation. Upon a second conviction the *minimum* sentence is to be seven years.

2. An improved Mark system.

3. Remission of a portion of the prisoner's sentence, to be earned by active exertions. The convict (after a prescribed course of probation,) to *work* his way out of prison by his industry; his general good conduct remaining an indispensable condition of release.

4. Supervision of Ticket-of-Leave men, who will have to report themselves to the head of the police of the district in which they reside once in every month; any police officer being authorized to bring a ticket-holder before a magistrate to answer to the charge of breaking the conditions of his license, which charge, when proved, will in all serious cases, lead to forfeiture, and even in minor cases to some imprisonment.

5. A distribution of photographic portraits to aid in the identification of released prisoners who may relapse into crime.

The Act of 1864 will tend to assimilate the English to the Irish System. But it appears that the new law makes no provision for the establishment in England of Intermediate Prisons—the most valuable portion and most interesting feature of the Irish System. Wanting this stage of Prison Discipline, it cannot be said that the Irish System will be fully or fairly on trial in England. English philanthropists hope, in the words of Mr. Hill, "that from an arch wanting comparatively so little to perfect it, the key-stone will not very long be withheld."

V. The Spanish Convict System.

Such has been the course of events in England and Ireland, since Americans have ceased their efforts to improve the discipline of prisons. But we have a confirmation of the principles so successfully acted upon in Ireland, in the experience of a country from which we should least expect it; I mean, Spain. The history of Colonel Montesinos and his model prison at Valencia is so instructive, that I will quote a part of it. My authorities are Colonel Montesinos himself, Captain Maconochie, already mentioned, Mr. Hoskins, a traveller in Spain, and Mr. M. D. Hill, the venerable Recorder of Birmingham, England.

The Public Prison at Valencia, when Don Manuel Montesinos was appointed its governor, in 1835, was a large, ill-arranged and filthy building, containing an average of one thousand prisoners, and sometimes as many as fifteen hundred. At that time the recommittals were from thirty to thirty-five per cent., which is about the same as in England and other European countries. For the years 1848–9–'50, according to

Captain Maconochie there were *no* recommittals, and for the ten years, 1838–'47, only an average of one per cent. How was this result secured? Mr. Recorder Hill, in a charge to the Grand Jury of Birmingham, makes the following statement:—

"In the city of Valencia there has long been a penitentiary gaol, under the government of Colonel Montesinos, a gentleman who has made for himself a European reputation, by his skill in the treatment of his prisoners. He acted upon them by urging them to self-reformation. He excited them to industry, by allowing them a small portion of their earnings for their own immediate expenditure, under due regulations to prevent abuse. He enabled them to raise their position, stage after stage, by their perseverance in good conduct. When they had acquired his confidence, he intrusted them with commissions, which carried them beyond the walls of their prison; relying on his moral influence which he had acquired over them to prevent their desertion. And finally he discharged them before the expiration of their sentences, when he had satisfied himself that they desired to do well, had acquired habits of patient labor, so much of skill in some useful occupation as would insure employment, the inestimable faculty of self-denial, the power of saying 'No' to the tempter, and, in short, such a general control over the infirmities of their minds and hearts as should enable them to deserve and maintain the liberty which they had earned. His success was answerable to the wisdom and zeal of his administration.

Colonel Montesinos is not now at the head of the prison of Valencia, having relinquished his office. By the system which he established, the prisoner was made aware that by behaving well, by applying himself to the acquisition of some art or trade, and by good moral conduct, he would ameliorate his present treatment and improve his future position; and *the desired result had been obtained of diminishing to two per cent. the annual recommitments, which had formerly amounted to thirty-five per cent.* The publication of the new penal code, which converted sentences of imprisonment for a long period of years into imprisonment for life, and which deprived the governor of all power of alleviating the condition of the convict, however much he may deserve it, or however desirable it might be as a stimulus to the others, took from the unhappy prisoner all hope that his industry or good conduct would avail him anything. Unconsoled by the hope of improving their lot, Colonel M. observed that the convicts lost their energy, a feeling of despair spread among them, and their ardor in acquiring a trade abated; indeed, *that they continued to work at all was the result of discipline and consequent subordination; but they labored without zeal, without any love of work,* and without the hearty good will they had exhibited before the introduction of the new penal code. Finding no means by which he could counteract this terrible evil, which utterly destroyed his system, Colonel M. resigned his appointment.

He had, moreover, another reason, namely, that the promulgation of the said code was followed by the appointment of incompetent persons as officers, who, faulty in character, and having other unfavorable qualities, could not produce good results."

"The same material organization remains in the prison of Valencia, but the spirit of his internal arrangements has disappeared since the Colonel departed, to such a degree that in the workshops scarcely any work is done, and what is accomplished is badly performed; the remarkable cleanliness and order which was formerly observed has disappeared; desertions, then so exceedingly rare, even of those who worked outside the walls, now amount to a most disgraceful number, so that there have been as many as forty-three convicts at once under heavy punishment for attempts to escape."

The Spanish Government, sensible of the great services of Colonel Montesinos, appointed him Inspector-General of Prisons for the kingdom, but unfortunately, the legislators of that country were not imbued with his wisdom. They established a new code, concerning which I will again quote Mr. Hill: —

"In the chapters of the new code which relate to the management of prisons, governors are prohibited from offering those encouragements to the prisoners which had raised them step by step until they were fitted for the enjoyment of liberty; and they also make it imperative that every sentence of imprisonment shall be fulfilled to the last hour. The combined effects of these innovations teem with instruction. Prisons which had been models of order and cleanliness, of cheerful industry and of praiseworthy demeanor in general, now exhibit a painful contrast to that happy state of things; they have become the scenes of indolence, disorder, and filth; and the prisoners are either reduced to despair or urged upon plots for escape, which, in a multitude of instances, are followed by success."

The following additional information is derived from Mr. Hill. Speaking of the discipline, he says: —

"Colonel Montesinos, in his written memoirs, says, when explaining and advocating a certain measure, 'the commandant who knew how to choose his officers would have no untoward events to lament in his prison,' which is proved by the fact that during the twenty years of his governorship of the prison of Valencia, he never needed an armed force for the guard within the walls, nor even for that which accompanied the gangs of prisoners who worked outside, amounting in number often to 400 men, for whom the convict officers were quite sufficient, and among whom there never were either plots or desertions.

" For each hundred persons is required an overseer, chosen from among retired sergeants in the army ; four *cabos primeros* and four *cabos segundos,* selected from among the prisoners. It will cause surprise that the criminals themselves should be employed as *cabos*, and should be permitted to exercise authority, but the experience of many years has proved the utility and economy of the arrangement ; its utility is shown in this, that selected with due discretion, the men are thoroughly acquainted with their companions, with whom they live in constant intercourse ; they understand their predilections and desires, are aware of their propensities, and foresee their actions, and thus are frequently able to avert the necessity of punishment. As they obtain consideration, besides deriving benefit in other ways, from their office, they endeavor to retain it by performing its duties well. Moreover, this arrangement affords a stimulus to the rest to behave well, that they may in their turn be promoted. From among these latter are chosen the *cabos 'segundos,'* and from these, according to the proofs of reformation and of repentance they give, and provided they are under light sentences for only slight offences, are selected individuals to replace the vacancies which may occur among the *cabos 'primeros.'* "

VI. The Bavarian Convict System.

I shall close these accounts of European prisons by some citations from a letter written in 1854, by the celebrated George Combe, of Edinburgh, describing the Bavarian prison at Munich, under the charge of Councillor Obermaier : —

" I have found here an unexpected illustration of the power of the moral sentiments and intellect to govern and reform criminals, without using the lash or any severe punishment, and also irrespective of all theory or system. Herr Regierungsrath Obermaier is the Governor of the Criminal Prison of this City, and has under his charge about 600 of the worst male convicts, collected from all the districts of Bavaria. Their sentences extend from eight to twelve years' imprisonment, and some of them for life. Their crimes have generally been attempts to murder, murder with extenuating circumstances, or highway robbery. A more unpromising set of convicts could hardly be imagined, and yet there are no separate cells, no severe discipline, no paid superintendents, except a turnkey to each ward, whose station is outside the door, and who does not see into the apartment.

"The prisoners are collected in workshops, to the number of ten, twenty, or thirty, according to the size of the room; for the prison is merely an old cloister, and they labor each in a trade, under the superintendence of one of themselves. They sleep in similar groups, and have each a separate bed, a straw mattress, two very clean white sheets, a pillow, and a white blanket. In the winter there is a large stove in each sleeping-room, and also in each workshop. They eat in common, take exercise in the yard in common, and, in short, are under no perceptible restraint, except the prison bars and walls, and look much more like men working quietly in different kinds of production, in a great manufactory, than a collection of desperate criminals undergoing penal sentences. They card wool and flax, spin both, dye the wool, weave both, and dress both the linen and woollen cloth, so as to complete them for use. There are tailors', carpenters', shoemakers,' and blacksmiths' workshops; and in none of them is any intelligence, except that of the convicts themselves, employed either to teach or superintend. The bars on the window are so slight, and so many tools are intrusted to the convicts, that escape could be easily accomplished, for outside there is only one soldier, and he cannot see a fourth of the windows; yet the culprits do not break the prison.

"Every prisoner," said Obermaier to Mr. Combe, "is brought before me on his entrance, and I converse with him. I ask him if his father or mother be alive; if he has a wife and children, brothers or sisters? and how they must feel degraded by his crime and sentence. I appeal to him through them; I tell him that I am his friend, not his enemy. That I regard him as sent to me to be reformed, and not merely to be punished. I explain to him the rules of the house, and tell him that they are all calculated for the improvement of the prisoners; that if he will be my friend, I shall be his; and that suffering and misery will overtake him here only in consequence of his own fault. The rudest natures," continued he, "can rarely resist such an appeal. The big tears often roll down cheeks that were never wet with weeping before, and I soon make them feel that my words are not speeches, but the expression of actual things. I give the new comer into the charge of the superintendent of the department for which he is most fitted, and recommend him to his care as his friend and adviser; and I appeal to the other men in his behalf.

"Should the new convict, as frequently happens, not believing in the reality of the law of kindness, begin to behave ill to his fellow-convicts, they soon check him and set him right. The public spirit among them is in favor of obedience and steady conduct, and they say to him, 'That conduct will not do here; Herr Von Obermaier is our friend, and we shall not allow you to act contrary to the rules of the house.'

"'But,' said I, 'at night are not all abominations practised, or how do you restrain them?' 'You see,' said he, 'that there is a space between each bed; an overseer, one of themselves, whom I can thoroughly trust, is on watch all night, with a bright light burning in every room, and every offence is observed and reported to me. I use persuasion with the offender—punish him by withholding part of his food, or depriving him of some other enjoyment—and he generally gives up his misconduct. When the general spirit of the men is directed towards virtue, an individual finds it extremely difficult to persevere in vice in the face of their condemnation.'"

Such, in the opinion of Mr. Combe and of Councillor Obermaier, were the beneficial features and results of the system pursued at Munich, that they ought to be introduced into all the prisons of Bavaria and England. But according to Professor Mittermaier, one of the highest authorities on the subject of Prison Discipline in Germany and throughout Europe, such has not been the opinion of the Bavarian Government. In a learned paper read before the Social Science Congress in 1862, Professor Mittermaier said:—

"In Bavaria, the opinion has been more and more gaining ground, that the associated system of imprisonment can hardly fail to act more or less injuriously on the convict, and can only to a certain point be reformatory. Even in the prison at Munich, in which Herr Obermaier labored so zealously, the increasing number of murders perpetrated among the convicts, especially of those suspected of being informers or traitors, showed that he himself was under illusion as to the success of his system. In Parliament, the old system was attacked, and the introduction of the Separate System demanded."

In compliance with these demands, by a law passed November 10th, 1861, the Bavarian Government has partially established the system of separate confinement. They extend it to men, but not to women, nor to convicts whose physical or mental strength appears unequal to it, and in no case beyond a period of five years. Those who show symptoms of amendment, after a year's separate confinement, are admitted to work with others, but it does not appear that there is any shortening of the period of sentence, as under the English and Irish systems.

VII. The General Tendency of Prison Reform in Europe.

From this synopsis which I have given of the prison systems of four countries, and from a general examination of the subject, I am led to believe that Prison Discipline is more carefully studied and better illustrated in Europe than in America, where, since the famous discussions of the Boston Prison Discipline Society, in 1846-7-8, but little public interest has been taken in the matter. The general tendency of both theory and practice in Europe is towards a union of the two conflicting systems which were then so warmly discussed in Massachusetts and throughout the country. The *Congregate* System, as here understood and practised, is almost discontinued in Europe; the *Separate* System, in its rigor, is more common, but in many countries, as in England and Ireland, it has been reduced to a subordinate, though still a very important, place in Prison Discipline. It is the introduction to associated labor, and the penalty of misconduct. With us it is often nominally so, but there is no such clear and definite and well applied function assigned to separate confinement among us, as we find in the Irish prisons.

But a still more noteworthy tendency in Europe is toward a remission of sentences, not by free pardon, which is almost always injurious, but through the consistent efforts of the convict himself. The system thus indicated applies moral and reasonable restraints and inducements, rather than those of force and routine, which are so natural to a prison. Of this system, it is claimed that Ireland furnishes a brilliant and successful example; and it is this system which I beg leave to present for your most earnest examination and consideration.

PART SECOND.

THE MASSACHUSETTS SYSTEM AND ITS RESULTS.

To bring before the General Court the exact character and results of our own system will best show the urgent necessity for its modification, if any better one can be devised. In what follows, I shall endeavor to demonstrate that our Penitentiaries and County Prisons are very costly ; that they do not effect, or even efficiently aid in the reformation of criminals ; and that it is very doubtful if they impose any considerable check upon crime. And I shall first consider what I regard as the least important of these defects in our system,.its great expense..

In my First Annual Report, already submitted to the General Court, by the Board of State Charities, I have set forth in some detail the expenses of the State Prison, and of the County Prisons for a period of years. To the tables there given, I would refer you for detailed confirmation of what I am now to state. I shall for the present, omit considering the State Prison, which, however, it should be said, corresponds in grade and object to the Irish prisons already described.

I. Great Increase in the Cost of County Prisons.

By an inspection of Table 83 in my Annual Report, it will be seen that the net cost of the County Prisons increased from $99,318.76 or $1.32.5 per week in 1853, to $202,426.21, or $3.43 per week in 1864, while the average number of prisoners was 322 less in 1864 than in 1853.

Here is an enormous increase of expense in eleven years ; no less than 150 per cent. on the average weekly cost, and more than 100 per cent. on the total cost of the prisons. To what must we ascribe it ?

No doubt it is partly due to the diminished number of male prisoners, who in most prisons earn the large share of the money received for labor. In part it is due to the increased cost of articles of consumption ; while the disproportionate increase in the average cost is in a small degree owing to the diminished average number. But none of these causes will account for such an unheard of addition to the county expenses.

Look next at the increase in Salaries, and the cost of Provisions, as compared with the earnings of Prison Labor.

Table I.

Showing the average cost to each prisoner, for eleven years (1854–1864) of Salaries, Provisions, and Earnings.

	1854.	1855.	1856.	1857.	1858.	1859.	1860.	1861.	1862.	1863.	1864.
Salaries,	$17 41	$19 09	$17 25	$20 76	$20 36	$26 53	$29 75	$30 49	$37 01	$43 25	$63 15
Provisions,	90 72	93 59	95 16	103 24	93 87	39 10	42 87	40 61	50 17	53 48	71 47
Labor,	33 50	26 69	28 96	32 53	29 47	33 28	30 79	23 26	27 91	31 75	30 29

In this table the cost of Provisions in the earlier years is set down as far greater than it actually was, being what was formerly returned as "Board of Prisoners." In the years 1855 and 1856 it is given as considerably more than the whole expenses. The real cost of Provisions was probably about two-fifths of what is here given for the years 1854–1858. But looking at the cost since 1858 a great advance appears; not less than 80 per cent.

It is in Salaries, however, that the costly nature of our present system can best be seen. In eleven years, if we may trust the returns, the salaries of officers in the county prisons have nearly trebled, while the average number of prisoners has fallen off nearly a quarter part; so that the *increase* in the average cost in salaries to each prisoner has been 250 per cent. since 1854. In other words, while the care and oversight of 1,455 prisoners cost but $25,000 in 1854, the care and oversight of 1,133 prisoners in 1864 cost $71,000. It is believed that no branch of the public service exhibits such a waste of the public money.

Not that I would blame the officers themselves for this state of things, or intimate that they do not perform their duties. But many of them have next to no duties to perform. Is it to be believed that the custody of fifteen prisoners in the Plymouth Prison requires the employment of officers whose salaries are $1,904.60; or that thirty prisoners in the Fitchburg Prison need be guarded at an expense of $3,070.51?

For the oversight of 2,866 persons in the town almshouses, $76,535.02 are paid; for the oversight of 1,850 persons in the State almshouses, $22,719 are paid; for the oversight of 1,133 prisoners in the county prisons, 177 officers are employed and

$71,686.55 are paid. It costs more than twice as much per man to guard and employ the prisoners than the town paupers, and more than five times as much than to guard, employ, and care for the State paupers at Tewksbury, Monson, and Bridgewater. Can any one believe that the labor or responsibility is five times as great? I am assured by an officer who has had long experience in both capacities, that the services of an almshouse officer are more irksome and difficult than those of a prison officer, and I can readily believe it.

The remedy for this extravagance in the employment of officers, is to classify and bring together the prisoners. We had on the first of October 1,074 prisoners scattered through fourteen counties, in no less than twenty-two different prisons; an average of less than fifty in each prison. 304 of these were in jails, and perhaps could not well be transferred beyond their county limits, though there need be only one jail in each county. But the 770 in Houses of Correction might just as well be transferred into three or four district prisons. One of these might be at South Boston, to receive the convicts of Suffolk, Norfolk, and a part of Worcester; another might be at Cambridge, for the convicts of Essex and Middlesex; another at New Bedford, for Bristol, Barnstable, Plymouth, Dukes, Nantucket, and a part of Worcester; and a fourth at Springfield, for the four western counties and the remainder of Worcester County.

Beside these, there might be a separate prison for boys, say at Greenfield, and another for women at Fitchburg or Ipswich.

All these changes could be made without building a single new cell in either of the prisons named.

II. The Albany Penitentiary.

The cost of salaries in these six district prisons need not exceed $30,000, or less than half what is now paid, and many of the other expenses could be diminished also. The Albany Penitentiary is such a district prison as I have described. For the year 1863, the average number of prisoners there was 377, and the total salaries about $8,000, or a little less than a third as great as the salaries in our county prisons.

The effect of this consolidation of prisons would be to make the labor of the prisoners twice as valuable. In the Albany

Penitentiary, just named, which differs but little from our Houses of Correction in the character and length of sentence of its convicts, their labor, together with the board of prisoners, has paid the expenses of the prison since its opening, and left a handsome profit over and above, of $36,141.54 in fourteen years, or something more than $2,500 a year. The constant average number of prisoners during this period was 228.05, of whom 64.74 were females, so that each convict, by the average, for the whole period, apparently earned about *eleven dollars* a year above the entire cost of his support in the prison.

It is true that the Albany Penitentiary is a remarkable instance of financial success in the management of convicts. It is under the control of an extraordinary man, General Pilsbury, the son of a celebrated Warden of the New Hampshire State Prison, and himself for many years famous as the Warden of the Connecticut State Prison, at Wethersfield. The same success attended his management at Wethersfield from 1828 to 1844. It is due in great measure to personal qualities, which he seems to have inherited, and which few prison officers can be expected to possess. But his system of economy and discipline, introduced in our prisons, if once consolidated, would show results which are now deemed unattainable. He has proved that County Prisons can be made to support themselves; and with his example before us, we ought not to continue to pay such extravagant sums for their support.*

We shall be told that the discipline of the Albany Penitentiary is not such as would be tolerated in Massachusetts; that the food and clothing of the convicts there are mean, and their labor excessive; that the practice of such frugality as General Pilsbury enforces is a wrong to the prisoners and disgraceful to the public. On the contrary, I think an inquiry would show that, though severe, this experienced officer is not inhuman, and that his theories concerning the food and clothing of convicts are very nearly correct. It is more doubtful whether his system tends more to reform criminals than the milder one pursued in Massachusetts. Both in his prison and in ours, however, the Auburn or *Congregate* System is nominally in use.

* See Appendix (B.)

The following Tables exhibit an abstract of the expenses, earnings and number of prisoners at the Albany Penitentiary, from 1850 to 1863, inclusive.

TABLE II.—THE ALBANY PENITENTIARY.

Showing the Whole Number, Average Number, etc., in confinement, from 1850–1863, with the average and total expenses.

YEARS.	Whole No in confinement during the year.	No. of males.	No. of females.	Average number of males in confinement.	Average number of females in confinement.	Total average.	Average weekly cost of each person.	Total expense.
1850, .	675	–	–	–	–	162	$1 21.9	$10,261 42
1851, .	774	542	232	120	54 2/3	174 2/3	1 22.6	11,138 92
1852, .	934	655	279	155 2/3	69 3/4	225 5/12	1 21.8	14,285 65
1853, .	950	692	258	170 5/6	68 2/3	239 1/2	1 20.7	15,038 12
1854, .	916	690	226	150 11/12	58 11/12	209 5/6	1 35.2	14,755 20
1855, .	1,031	769	262	158 11/12	64 11/12	223 5/6	1 33.9	15,587 72
1856, .	1,203	887	316	155 1/12	55 5/6	210 11/12	1 38.2	15,167 94
1857, .	1,434	1,084	350	194	65 5/12	259 5/12	1 40.4	18,945 49
1858, .	1,414	1,079	335	199 1/3	66 5/6	266 1/6	1 33.1	18,434 36
1859, .	1,460	1,136	324	187 5/12	69 11/12	257 1/3	1 01.3	13,562 45
1860, .	1,726	1,360	366	184 1/12	65 1/3	249 5/12	1 10.3	14,316 71
1861, .	1,793	1,357	436	185 1/2	76 5/6	262 1/3	1 04.7	14,295 26
1862, .	1,320	912	408	154	82 1/4	236 1/4	1 19.3	14,661 17
1863, .	1,470	991	479	270 3/4	106 10/12	377 7/12	1 24.4	24,524 60
Total,	17,100	12,154	4,271	2,286 1/2	906 1/6	3,192 2/3	$1 29.4	$214,975 01

TABLE III.—THE ALBANY PENITENTIARY.

Showing the Average Expenses per inmate, (1850–1863.)

YEARS.	Average number of convicts.	Improvements and repairs.	Furniture.	Clothing and bedding.	Provisions.	General expense for each person.	Total expense of each person.
1850, . .	162	$2 20.5	$1 03	$4 08	$29 57.6	$26 44.8	$63 34.2
1851, . .	174⅔	78.2	1 62.1	4 83.3	30 72.8	25 80.5	63 77.2
1852, . .	225 5/12	81.0	2 39.8	4 38.6	28 75.5	27 02.6	63 37.4
1853, . .	239½	1 27.6	1 50.6	4 69.6	29 00.4	26 30.4	62 37.2
1854, . .	209⅚	5 67.8	1 67.4	3 43	31 74.8	27 78.5	70 31.8
1855, . .	223⅚	2 45.3	70.3	4 30	35 05	27 13	69 71.4
1856, . .	210 11/12	1 76.3	1 09.6	4 94.2	33 76.4	30 34.7	71 91.4
1857, . .	259 5/12	1 53.8	1 67.9	3 46.4	36 16.9	30 17.8	73 03.1
1858, . .	266⅙	4 00.8	1 35.8	5 22.7	29 72.3	28 94	69 25.8
1859, . .	257⅓	73.5	1 63.6	3 87.8	24 09.6	22 35.6	52 70.3
1860, . .	249 5/12	1 13.9	2 59.3	3 94.6	24 88	24 84	57 40
1861, . .	262⅓	1 94	1 36.8	3 14.4	24 34.6	23 70.5	54 49.2
1862, . .	236¼	2 65.1	1 78.7	2 86.7	28 61.2	26 13.9	62 05.7
1863, . .	377 7/12	2 42.8	2 23.7	6 53.1	31 26.2	22 46.9	64 95.1
Averages,	3,192⅔	$2 12.5	$1 75	$4 56.8	$27 95.3	$27 51.5	$67 33.3

TABLE IV.—THE ALBANY PENITENTIARY.

Showing the average income per inmate, and from what sources derived.

YEARS.	Basket & Wood-work Shop.	Shoemaking.	Chair-Shop.	Demijohn, Hardware & Smith Shop.	Female Department.	Board Account.	Visitors & Fines.	Interest Account.	Total average Income.	Average Deficit.	Average Excess.
1850,	$4 73.4	$1 43.6	$15 39.7	$17 39.4	$4 23.9	$14 79.8	$2 26.3	$0 29.3	$60 55.2	$2 78.3	—
1851,	6 89.5	1 36.4	23 40.8	14 58.1	7 25.1	13 65.7	1 65.7	75.9	69 57.2	—	$5 80
1852,	7 90.6	71.2	25 91.1	16 41.6	10 67.4	12 48.9	2 62.4	46.5	73 62.2	—	10 24.7
1853,	6 28.2	—	42 84.3	—	11 46.7	13 79.6	1 25.4	—	75 64.5	—	12 85.6
1854,	7 72.4	—	41 19.5	1 46.5	11 67.8	13 09.7	2 04.9	—	77 68.2	—	7 36.4
1855,	4 00.3	—	20 30.6	28 86.1	9 27.4	16 35.9	2 34.6	43.7	81 19.5	—	11 55.5
1856,	2 93	—	19 73	31 69.7	10 31.8	16 80.7	2 49.7	—	86 98.2	—	15 06.7
1857,	3 29.1	—	19 50.1	28 47.2	7 62.3	19 80.7	2 31.4	—	81 32.9	—	8 29.7
1858,	—	4 57.7	5 93.5	2 98	2 79.1	20 12.5	53	—	31 73.5	37 52.3	—
1859,	91.9	33 94	6 69.4	—	8 84.7	13 62.5	1 88.4	—	70 41	—	17 70.7
1860,	1 30.5	37 95.7	6 18.2	—	8 09.3	17 73.8	3 23.4	17.2	73 72.3	—	16 32.2
1861,	1 39.9	26 75	5 32.9	—	6 25.4	16 85.5	2 63.7	13.8	58 48.7	—	3 99.5
1862,	70.2	37 68.8	3 52.5	—	12 93.8	16 64	1 51.9	—	76 93.6	—	14 87.8
1863,	—	58 79	38.7	—	10 10.2	21 12.6	1 05.2	—	111 36.3	—	46 32.3
Averages,	$3 24.5	$18 22	$16 38.9	$10 51.3	$9 18.7	$20 06.3	$2 04.7	$0 14.2	$78 65.4	—	$11 33

TABLE V.—THE ALBANY PENITENTIARY.

Showing the Expenditures and Income for the years from 1850 to 1863, inclusive.

YEARS.	Improvements and Repairs.	EXPENDITURES.				Total Expense.
		Furniture.	Clothing and Bedding.	Provisions.	General Expense Account.	
1850,	$357 29	$166 98	$661 01	$4,791 42	$4,284 72	$10,261 41
1851,	136 71	283 19	844 24	5,367 34	4,507 44	11,138 92
1852,	182 72	540 82	988 72	6,481 18	6,092 21	14,285 65
1853,	305 84	360 87	1,124 92	6,946 66	6,299 83	15,038 12
1854,	1,191 63*	351 32	720 13	6,661 79	5,830 33	14,755 20
1855,	549 10	157 56	962 86	7,845 56	6,072 64	15,587 72
1856,	371 93	231 20	1,042 42	7,121 60	6,400 79	15,167 94
1857,	399 24	435 59	898 77	9,383 10	7,828 79	18,945 49
1858,	1,067 05*	361 62	1,391 29	7,911 48	7,702 92	18,434 36
1859,	189 21	421 16	997 94	6,200 96	5,753 18	13,562 45
1860,	284 15	646 96	984 20	6,205 73	6,195 67	14,316 71
1861,	509 07	355 58	825 03	6,386 80	6,218 78	14,295 26
1862,	626 47	422 23	677 45	6,759 62	6,175 40	14,661 17
1863,	917 05	853 12	2,466 06	11,804 36	8,484 01	24,524 60
Total,	$6,787 46	$5,558 20	$14,585 04	$89,247 60	$87,846 71	$214,975 00

* Including building account.

TABLE V.—Concluded.

INCOME.

YEARS.	Basket and Wood-work Shop.	Shoe Shop.	Chair Shop.	Demijohn, Hardware and Smith Shop.	Female Department.	Board Account.	Visitors and Fines.	Interest Account.	Total Income.	Earnings.
1850,	$767 00	$232 72	$2,494 40	*$2,817 96	$686 86	$2,397 41	$366 68	$47 48	$9,810 51	$$450 91
1851,	1,204 43	238 28	4,088 72	*2,546 85	1,266 58	2,384 87	289 55	132 71	12,151 99	1,013 07
1852,	1,782 26	160 71	5,842 52	*2,867 23	2,406 17	2,815 33	616 61	104 88	16,595 71	2,310 06
1853,	1,504 56		10,260 95	—	2,747 00	3,304 20	300 47		18,117 18	3,079 06
1854,	1,620 88		8,650 93	†307 52	2,450 77	2,748 39	430 13	91 80	16,300 42	1,545 22
1855,	896 02		4,545 31	‡6,460 24	2,075 85	3,661 70	525 13		18,174 25	2,586 53
1856,	618 10		4,161 49	‡6,685 51	2,176 30	4,177 76	526 82		18,345 98	3,178 04
1857,	853 77		5,059 06	‡7,386 16	1,977 78	5,221 00	600 48		21,098 25	2,152 76
1858,	244 68	1,218 46	1,579 69	‡793 32	742 98	3,626 63	141 09		8,446 85	$9,987 51
1859,	335 93	8,734 01	1,722 69		2,276 78	4,564 83	484 82		18,119 06	4,556 61
1860,	348 94	9,467 27	1,542 06		2,018 71	4,204 10	806 82		18,387 90	4,071 19
1861,	184 38	7,017 56	1,398 22		1,640 66	4,365 38	691 79	45 34	15,343 33	1,048 07
1862,	—	8,904 02	832 90		3,056 41	4,991 21	359 04	32 72	18,176 30	3,515 13
1863,	—	22,198 47	146 41		3,814 48	15,492 16	397 30		42,048 82	17,524 22
Total,	$10,360 95	$58,171 50	$52,325 35	$33,564 79	$29,337 33	$64,054 97	$6,536 73	$454 93	$251,116 55	$36,141 54

* Demijohn shop. † Hardware shop. ‡ Hardware and Smith shop. § Deficit.

The average length of sentence of the prisoners at Albany seems to be about four months; in our Houses of Correction, it will probably average as long. In some it is much more, in others much less. This is an important element in all calculations respecting prison labor; a short sentence making a prisoner almost useless for any purposes of labor. The age of the Albany prisoners is probably a little greater than that of ours. In other respects the comparison is a tolerably fair one. The earnings at Albany, however have been swelled of late years by the sums paid for the board of United States prisoners, which do not appear in our own prison returns.

III. The Expense of our Jails.

Our County Prisons generally include both a Jail and a House of Correction under the same roof. The distinction between the two is this; there are none but convicts in the House of Correction, and all are *obliged* to labor; in the Jails there are a few convicts, a few debtors, a few witnesses, and a great many persons waiting trial; and none of these are *obliged* to labor. Of course the expenses of the Jails must be much greater in proportion to the average number than those of the Houses of Correction.

I have not attempted to separate these expenses when the two institutions are combined, though this has sometimes been done in former years; because all such calculations must rest very much upon conjecture. The Boston Jail alone contains about half the whole number and half the average number of all committed during the year. The average weekly cost in this Jail for the past year is almost exactly that of the whole State for both Jails and Houses of Correction. I do not know that these jail expenses can be very much reduced, but it is a matter worthy of inquiry.

IV. Labor in the Houses of Correction.

That the expenses of the Houses of Correction can be much diminished by a better organization of the labor of prisoners, can hardly be doubted. The average earnings of the convicts at Albany for 1863 were nearly $70; at the South Boston House of Correction during the year 1864, a little above $70; but in all the Houses of Correction taken together only about $41 for each prisoner of the average, or less than two-thirds of what it might be. It is true that the figures as returned, do not accurately show the value of the prison labor to the counties ; at Ipswich, for example, the average value of labor is only set down as $20.30 ; while it probably was nearly double that. But after making all allowance for such defects in the return, the value of our prison labor in the Houses of Correction is not more than two-thirds what it might be, under a system of consolidation and classification of prisons. Nor would the health of the convicts suffer by exacting a third more work than they now do, generally speaking.

It is not, however, because the convicts do not work, as a rule, that the receipts from labor are so small ; but because their labor is not well remunerated. In the Dedham House of Correction, with an average of sixty-one prisoners, no profit whatever is received from labor ; at Barnstable, at Lenox, Northampton, Lawrence, and several other places the profit is very small, because either the number of convicts is small, or the work done ill paid, or a want of enterprise in the management of the shops keeps down the earnings. If a single Inspector had authority to make contracts for all the prison labor in the country, he could largely increase its profits.

I have no doubt, also, that the prison labor at Charlestown might be made much more profitable.

To sum up then, our prisons are costly ; they are yearly increasing in expense ; they are too many in number, and too fully officered ; and they do not economically employ the labor of their inmates. If with all their financial defects, they prevented crime and reformed their inmates, we should not, perhaps, complain, although the most frugal management is often the most humane and intelligent. But I fear they cannot be allowed either of these merits.

V. Our Prisons do not Diminish Crime.

Perhaps I shall be told, " But the statistics show that crime in Massachusetts is on the decline ; in 1855 there were seventeen thousand four hundred and fifty-seven commitments to the county prisons, in 1864 less than ten thousand ; in 1858 the average number in those prisons was one thousand nine hundred and fifty-seven, and in the State Prison four hundred and sixty-nine, while this year you report only one thousand one hundred and thirty-three in the former, and three hundred and seventy-seven in the latter. Is not this a great falling off? and shall not our prisons have the credit of it, at least in part?"

To this I should answer, " The causes which have diminished commitments are various, but none of them can be traced to the terrors or the reformatory character of our prisons."

In part, this decrease is only apparent, resulting (in the case of the county prisons,) from exaggerated returns (as I believe,) in former years. The great cause of the decrease in obvious crime, however, is the war, and the demand for labor which it has occasioned. So closely are crime and pauperism allied, that what increases one increases both. Then it is beyond question that hundreds of our habitual criminals, who were often in prison for grave or light offences, have gone to the war. On the return of peace, we shall find our prisons filling up again; especially, if there should be any depression of business in consequence of a deranged currency.

It is common to test the efficacy of prisons by the re-committals, although in a country like ours, where men readily pass from one jurisdiction to another, this is a very uncertain test. Applying this we shall see what claim our prisons can make that they have repressed crime.*

By the official returns it appears that in 1854 twenty-one per cent. of all committed to our Houses of Correction were recommitments,—about a fifth part.

In 1862 the recommitments were fifty per cent., or half; in 1863, fifty-four per cent., and in seven months of 1864, nearly fifty-seven per cent. The Jails show a corresponding increase, but more surprising.

In 1854, the reported recommitments were a little more than one per cent.; in 1862, forty-two per cent.; in 1863, forty-five per cent.; in seven months of 1864, forty-two per cent. In the State Prison there is no regular increase or decrease.

These facts will appear by the following table:

* See Appendix (C.)

Table VI.—Recommitments.

Showing the Whole Number of Commitments, the Recommitments, and the percentage in the County Prisons and the State Prison since 1853.

YEARS.	Houses of Correction.			Jails.			State Prison.		
	Whole No.	Recommitted.	Per cent.	Whole No.	Recommitted.	Per cent.	Whole No.	Recommitted.	Per cent.
1854,	4,734	1,064	21	11,526	139	1.2	149	34	23.1
1855,	4,599	964	21	12,858	177	1.4	141	17	12.1
1856,	4,936	938	20	9,419	570	6	139	24	17.3
1857,	5,169	1,329	26	7,903	2,029	25	160	21	13.1
1858,	5,996	1,281	22	8,603	1,824	21	198	31	15.6
1859,	5,180	1,682	32	8,286	2,867	35	163	24	14.7
1860,	5,012	2,346	47	6,752	2,633	39	144	14	9.7
1861,	5,424	2.504	46	5,693	2,206	39	197	21	10.7
1862,	4,494	2,241	50	5,211	2,220	42	102	20	19.6
1863,	3,823	2,072	54	5,568	2,523	45	108	16	14.8
1864,*	1,780	1,017	57	2,801	1,167	42	79	10	12.6

* Seven months.

Of course, these figures for the County Prisons are wretchedly erroneous for the earlier years, but the steady increase in the recommitments, and the large percentage now existing, show that imperfect returns must not bear all the blame. There can be no manner of doubt that the recommitments to our prisons are very numerous, and that they have increased of late years, while crime in general has decreased.

If we look at some of the Houses of Correction this year, the case is still worse. Out of 211 committed in New Bedford since March 1st, 141, or about 70 per cent., are recommitments; out of 250 committed at South Boston, 237, or 94 per cent., are recommitments. Is it possible to believe that such prisons check crime?

VI. Our Prisons Considered as Schools of Reform.

But do our prisons work reformation of the criminal? The question has already been answered by the figures just given; but there are other means of answering it. Go to our prisons as I have done the past year, inquire of the officers, hear the story of the convicts, watch the workings of the system, and you will see that instead of reforming, they harden the criminal. Since the first of March last, 239 boys and girls, under fifteen, have been committed to our Jails, and 95 to our Houses of Correction. Of these 334, probably thirty appeared both in Jail and in the House of Correction, so that 300 would be about the number imprisoned in seven months, or at the rate of 500 a year. Of all these, if we can trust the opinion of the prison officers, scarcely one is morally benefited by his imprisonment, while the great majority are made worse by it. Among them are mere infants, almost, such as one whom I found in the Plymouth House of Correction, sentenced to thirty days imprisonment,—and he only *six years old.*

To show how our prison discipline corrects these boys, let me cite the case of one at Dedham. I visited the House of Correction there on Friday, the 30th of September last. The Tuesday noon before, this lad had been discharged from a first imprisonment of thirty days, and on Wednesday night he was brought back under a sentence of six months for stealing. This is, perhaps, a strong instance, but there are many pointing the same way; the House of Correction, as a rule, ruins more children than it reforms. Among the older criminals, there are some, no doubt, who are reformed, at least temporarily, but not enough, I am convinced, to balance the mischief done to young offenders. It is notorious how useless imprisonment is to reform female offenders.

At the State Prison, it may be that permanent reform is accomplished, in individual cases, but they are rare ones, in spite of the humanity, the wisdom and the diligence of the authorities there.

VII. Four Tests of our System.

I suppose there are four tests and only four, by which to judge any mode of prison discipline. The questions to be asked are these:—

1. Does it secure the *custody* of the convict?
2. Does it pay its own expenses?
3. Does it check and diminish crime?
4. Does it reform the criminal?

I have arranged these tests in order of their moral importance, the most important last. Of course, however, all the three subsequent ones depend upon the first; if prisons are not secure, they are useless for any purpose. I believe that our prisons are places of secure custody, and so far our system succeeds.

But I have endeavored to show that it secures neither of the other three objects of imprisonment; and, therefore, so far as concerns them, it is a failure. If this is admitted, (though I neither expect nor desire it to be admitted without further examination,) where does the fault lie, and how can it be remedied? I have pointed out a means of reducing our expenditures, but how can the more essential ends of prison discipline be gained?

VIII. Classifications and Conditional Remissions.

A partial answer to this latter question is found in the Irish system. The first step is *Classification*, the second *Conditional Remission*.

By Classification is meant, *first*, the separation of the sexes, and the removal of juvenile offenders from the contamination of their elders in crime; and, *second*, the formation of classes based on moral distinctions, in which the convict can place himself, and through which he can be promoted, step by step, until finally it will be safe to obliterate the hateful distinction by which he is known, and to restore him to that society of his fellows which he justly forfeited, but is now worthy to enjoy again. This is aimed at, and this, I venture to say, is done in Ireland. It can be equally well done here. Indeed, we have some great advantages over Ireland in such an experiment, which may be here mentioned.

1. We have no such large class of *habitual criminals* as is found in the British Isles, although they generously supply us every year from their abundance.

2. The moral tone of our people is much more favorable to such enlightened modes of procedure.

3. The demand for labor is much greater, and the avenues and careers of life much more open here to a penitent criminal than in older countries, where the lines of caste are more strongly drawn.

4. The character and abilities of our prison officers are said to be much higher than of those who hold such positions in

Europe. This was the testimony of M. De Tocqueville thirty years ago, and it is the opinion of Dr. Howe to-day.

At present we have scarcely the rudest semblance of classification. The State Prison is the only one of our forty prisons to which women are not sent; there is nowhere a special prison for females, nor for boys. Still less do we attempt any classification on moral grounds. But we have the means of both modes of classifying ready to our hand, as I have already intimated, and I respectfully suggest that some steps be taken towards this most desirable end.

Conditional Remission, or an alleviation of the sentence of a criminal in consideration for good behavior, is already a part of our code. But it might be made far more efficient and active, as a means of reformation. Wherever tried, it has worked well, and it ought now to be extended and developed into a system. In my account of the Irish prisons, I have indicated one form of such a system; ours must vary somewhat from that, and I hope we could make some improvements.

IX. Habitual Criminals.

First of all, however, we should recognize a class of habitual criminals, and adapt our penal laws to their condition. It is a mockery of reason and justice to deal with confirmed rascals as if they were young offenders; short sentences should be given up for such persons, and a term of imprisonment assigned which would give a reformatory discipline time enough to work in. This is the opinion of Sir Walter Crofton, of Captain Maconochie, and of all those in England and Ireland who have studied the habits of the criminal class. The number of this class is much smaller among us than in those countries, but its essential nature is the same everywhere, and there is need everywhere of the same discipline to correct it. There are plenty of instances in our county prisons, of persons who are committed twice, thrice, and even six times in a year, on short sentences. Of course it would be better for them, better for the community, and better for the prison, if their sentence were made a year instead of three months,—or even a period of years, if they belonged unmistakably to the class of criminals.

A change in the law regulating sentences, so as to double or treble their length, would much reduce the recommittals, at first, and if accompanied by a reformed method of prison discipline, would, perhaps, make the reduction permanent. Such a change as this would make it much more feasible to introduce the Irish system into county prisons, to which, in some respects, it is ill adapted. For it should be said that the prisons where this system has been mainly tried, were of the same class as our State Prison at Charlestown.

X. Classification must be Thorough.

In pointing out the need and the benefits of classification in our prisons, it should be added that these classes must be very carefully made, and very thoroughly kept up. Not only should we have separate prisons for the women, and for the young offenders, but a distinction should be made between second and third comers, and those sent for a first offence ; and between prisoners in different stages of their punishment. On this latter point I find some valuable suggestions in a letter to an English newspaper, by Mr. C. P. Measor, an officer at the Chatham Prison, from whom I have already quoted. Mr. Measor, writing January 2, 1865, says:—

"The very fact that convicts under their first, second, third, or fourth convictions, are indiscriminately mixed together throughout their entire sentences, is in itself a proof that the system must be most feebly reformatory, and that with an apparent attempt at order, the most confusing elements neutralize good results. A certain amount of association between prisoners under secondary punishment, is indispensable; but either let the claim to a reformatory effect in the system be abandoned, or the absurdly counteracting influence be prevented, which results from the letting in upon convicts who have attained a certain improvement by discipline and training, a constant flood of more recent depravity. In the world, we expect a moderate allowance of tares with the wheat; but if the best of us were condemned for years to almost entire 'evil communication,' we might fairly predict what would become of our 'manners.' These relays of fresh criminals, bringing with them from the outer world the latest news of events and old companions, and at the same time their own novel experiences, deprive a penal sentence of half its seclusion and nearly all its reformatory value. Irrespective of the great peril to the order of the convict prisons, the effect of thus jumbling up together those who are beginning and those who are ending their sentences—novices in crime and those who have been oft convicted, as well as the moderately good with the irreclaimably bad—may well be imagined.

"What is requisite for the management I have suggested is a constructional arrangement which shall enable the convicts, throughout their sentences, to be dealt with in fifties or hundreds, so that those convicted within the same few months shall neither have an opportunity of learning the prison experiences of their predecessors, nor be enlightened by the stirring incidents of subsequently convicted pals, bringing with them the latest dodges of the criminal profession. It is also indispensable that there should be a distinct establishment for life-sentenced men, as well as one for the reconvicted and incorrigible."

Such a classification as is here indicated, and by which criminals could be treated more as individuals and less in the mass, could easily be made in our present prisons, with very little alteration in their structure. The opposite method is that which prevails now both here and in England, and of this Mr. Measor says:—

"As long as convicts are treated upon a kind of regimental system—and all the order and plan which prevails in our prisons is of that kind—which merely appeals to the eye in certain disciplinary evolutions on the parade-ground, in meal-serving, in standing like sentries at each man's cell door, in marching to and from the public works, and in the decorous externals of congregational worship and psalmody, so long will it be impossible to arrive at any correct knowledge of their true character, to test their glib professions, or discriminate by any safe rule between the better and the worse.

"The plan of treating criminals 'en bloc,' and training them with military exactitude, rather than in reference to their dispositions, industry, and labor, has proved a signal failure; and in adopting a change, it should be an honest and a complete one.

"It may be thought by some that the subdivision and more accurate classification of convicts, must necessitate greater expense in their supervision.

"On the other hand, it would tend as much to economy as to their trial and improvement. Wherever large bodies of all kinds of criminals are associated without discrimination, the pressure of restraint requisite for the whole body is regulated by its weakest part. The same direct coercion which is necessary for a convict for the first year of his punishment ought not to be necessary in the second, and still less in the third, unless he be a very bad specimen of his class; for it must be a thorough condemnation of any so-called 'system,' if after a year or so it does not discriminate between those who require constant supervision and control, and those for whom they can be dispensed with."

That these observations are just, I believe the experience of our prisons, as well as those of England and Ireland will confirm.

XI. THE INSTRUCTION OF PRISONERS.

Such a classification as I have proposed would afford far greater facilities than now exist for the instruction of convicts, —a duty which, under our present arrangements, is greatly neglected, and yet is of the highest consequence.

The extent to which crime is connected with imperfect education, even here in Massachusetts, is not generally known. Something more than a third part of all persons committed to the prisons here can neither read nor write, and the great majority of the rest know little beyond that. It has been customary, in the returns of former years, to indicate the number of all committed who could not read and write, and the number born in Massachusetts who could not; but previous to 1857, a return was made of those who *could* read and write. This change in the mode of making the return introduces confusion into the statistics, and causes the number before 1857 who could not read and write, to appear much larger than it really was. For the past year, or since March 1, 1864, I have obtained returns classified differently. Those who could not read and write were entered as having *no* education; those who could read and write, and who had not been taught beyond the common branches, as having a common school education; and those who had been further instructed, as having a superior education. Out of 5,694 persons, 2,150 are reported as having no education—about 38 per cent.; 312, or about $5\frac{1}{2}$ per cent., as being able merely to read and write; 3,195, or about 56 per cent., as having a common school education; and only 37, or less than one per cent., as having a superior education.

I have reason to believe that these returns are more precise than they have been in former years, but it will be seen by the annexed table, that the proportion of those who could not read and write, for ten years preceding, has not been less than this, as shown by the returns. The returns for 1854–5–6, must be understood as very much exaggerated, for the reason already mentioned.

TABLE VII.—EDUCATION OF PRISONERS.

Showing the whole number, and the percentage to the whole number committed, of all Prisoners who could not read and write, in the County Prisons, 1854—1864.

YEARS.	Whole No. Reported.	Could not Read and Write.	Per cent.	YEARS.	Whole No. Reported.	Could not Read and Write.	Per cent.
1854, . .	16,260	11,991	73.7	1860, . .	11,764	3,708	31.5
1855, . .	17,457	13,023	74.6	1861, . .	11,117	3,702	33.3
1856, . .	14,355	9,656	67.3	1862, . .	9,705	1,965	20.2
1857, . .	13,072	4,853	37.1	1863, . .	9,391	3,312	35.3
1858, . .	14,599	6,534	44.7	1864, . .	5,694	2,150	37.8
1859, . .	13,466	4,493	33.4				

It seems probable, therefore, that at least two-fifths of all persons committed to our county prisons are either wholly uneducated, or have such a scanty knowledge of books that they cannot read the Bibles with which they are, from time to time, supplied. These figures may well startle us, for if we compare them with the corresponding statistics for the British Islands, where general education is much less attended to than in Massachusetts, we shall find the condition of our prison population almost as bad in this respect as that of England and Ireland, and apparently worse than that of Scotland. For it appears by official returns, that the proportion of all offenders in England and Wales, who cannot read or write, is only about 33 per cent., while in Ireland it is less than 50 per cent., and in Scotland not more than 25 per cent.

In the light of these facts and comparisons, it may well be asked what we are doing for the instruction of these regiments of untaught criminals. The returns given in my Annual Report will show that the sum actually returned as paid for instruction

1865.]   SENATE—No. 74.   73

in the last year was only $3,545.09, or at the rate of about three dollars for each prisoner of the average number. When it is remembered that this sum probably includes, in most prisons, the religious as well as the secular instruction, it will at once be seen how inadequate is the provision made in this particular. The average cost of provisions for each prisoner being upwards of *seventy-one* dollars, it will be at once manifest that our prisoners are "better fed than taught," in the ratio of at least twenty to one.

It is hardly necessary to enlarge on the importance of education as a check upon crime, but I will here quote the remarks of Mr. Neison, an eminent English statistician, who has given much attention to this particular topic. Mr. Neison observes:—

"It would seem that the evidence furnished of education, among even the criminals themselves, tends to show that the small amount of instruction implied in the test here recognized—the simple distinction between the ability to read and write imperfectly, and inability either to read or write at all—has a most material influence in the development of crime; and, were the investigation carried no further, we should be forced to conclude that, since the most criminal districts show a higher ratio of uninstructed persons among the criminals, and the less criminal districts a less proportion who are wholly destitute of the rudest elements of education, the immediate inference is, that even this small degree of instruction tends to the repression of crime."

I have already quoted the evidence and opinions of Mr. Measor, a high officer in one of the large English prisons. This gentleman has also offered some valuable suggestions relating to the schooling of convicts. "He suggested evening schooling three times a week, with the addition of occasional lectures, by duly qualified persons, upon subjects within the scope of ordinary minds. Mr. Measor said he would eliminate religion from ordinary school instruction in convict prisons, reward progress in solid and useful secular acquirements, and let the chaplains have their own separate classes or arrangements for religious teaching." The great test of a suitable education for convicts, he thinks, should be its utility in life. It should demonstrate that honesty is the best policy, impressing them with the policy of self-interest, and embracing all common subjects and pursuits.

There can be no doubt that in carrying out this, or any other plan of systematic instruction in our prisons, private benevolence would be found to assist cheerfully, and to great advantage. I had the pleasure of attending a religious service in the prison at Springfield, where the chaplain was assisted by several gentlemen of that city, and where the sheriff of the county also took part. It is to be wished that such a truly Christian spirit should be awakened everywhere; that such missionary work would be the rule, and not the exception, in our prisons. The example of Sarah Martin, the poor English dressmaker, who for many years, at her own expense, undertook the instruction of the prisoners in Yarmouth jail, might incite to similar efforts in a community whose boast it is that education is made universal, but which does little or nothing for the three or four thousand prisoners who can neither read nor write.

XII. Discharged Prisoners.

Closely connected with this subject of instructing prisoners, while in confinement, is the matter of aid to those discharged, and systematic efforts for their employment. Very little is now done in this direction, although the State employs an agent to look after discharged convicts, especially those from the State Prison. That the labors of this agent are faithfully rendered and within a limited field, effective, I doubt not. But the true field for such efforts is in the Houses of Correction, where the number of discharged convicts, and of recommitments is much greater than at the State Prison. The whole number of such discharges for the year ending October 1, 1864, was between three thousand and three thousand five hundred, while the discharges from the Jails after deducting the persons transferred to the State Prison, the Houses of Correction and the Reform Schools have been between four thousand and four thousand five hundred. The amount of aid furnished at the expense of the counties for this whole number of persons, is reported as $908.68; which was mostly expended in paying their fares home. An average assistance of *twelve cents apiece* cannot have advanced these convicts far on the road to comfort or virtue. Probably much more was done for them by benevolent individuals, and there has been organized during the year 1864 a society of ladies to found an institution under the name of *The Temporary Asylum for Discharged Female Prisoners,* which, it is believed, will do much to provide for this class of criminals. These ladies opened their asylum in the month of December, at Dedham, and have already received several inmates.. Their labors, however, include an examination of the prisons, also, and they will be able to reach many cases which never come within their modest establishment. From this beginning much good may be expected to come, and it is to be hoped that something like the Female Refuges in England and Ireland may be established among us as a part of our prison system.

The Board of State Charities, in their Report have already commended this organization to the favorable notice of the Legislature. I would beg leave to add that in any modification of our prison system, it might be worthy of consideration whether such Asylums or Refuges should not be directly encouraged by an annual grant of money.

If, as I continue to hope, Massachusetts shall, after due examination, adopt the better features of the Irish System, the employment and supervision of discharged prisoners will become an important concern of our prison officers. Whenever this is done, I have the best expectations of the good thence resulting, knowing, as I do, the general high character, good sense and humanity of those officers. Even now they do much to supply the defects of a very imperfect system.

XIII. INCREASE OF CRIME AMONG FEMALES AND MINORS.

In this connection it may be well to notice the steady increase of crime among females during the last ten years; an increase which is not only relatively large, because the number of male criminals has decreased, but is absolutely considerable, amounting in some prisons to double what it was before the war began. It is undoubtedly connected with the war; the absence of male relatives giving room for greater temptations, and, in many instances, the receipt of bounty money or State Aid increasing the tendency to intemperance and a profligate life. This state of things sets in a stronger light the necessity which has long existed for a separate female prison, with female officers, and under regulations differing somewhat from those of the male prisons. As has been noticed, separate prisons of this kind exist in England and Ireland ; they are also found in New York, and perhaps in other States of the Union. The constant proportionate increase of crime among females can be seen by the following table which is made up from the annual returns. Though evidently erroneous in some respects, it will show the general tendency since 1853 accurately enough.

TABLE VIII.

Showing the number of Male and Female Prisoners committed to the County Prisons, for eleven years, 1854 to 1864, inclusive.

YEARS.	JAILS.			HOUSES OF CORRECTION.			TOTALS.		
	Whole No. committed.	Males.	Females.	Whole No. committed.	Males.	Females.	Whole No. committed.	Males.	Females.
1854, .	11,526	9,819	1,652	4,734	3,735	999	16,260	13,604	2,651
1855, .	12,858	10,819	2,026	4,599	3,550	1,048	17,457	14,369	3,074
1856, .	9,419	8,775	626	4,936	3,840	1,090	14,355	12,615	1,716
1857, .	7,903	6,675	1,228	5,169	3,974	1,195	13,072	10,649	2,423
1858, .	8,603	7,390	1,213	5,996	4,660	1,336	14,599	12,050	2,549
1859, .	8,286	6,716	1,579	5,180	4,113	1,089	13,466	10,829	2,668
1860, .	6,752	5,756	1,031	5,012	4,000	1,012	11,764	9,756	2,043
1861, .	5,693	4,689	1,013	5,424	4,322	1,154	11,117	9,011	2,167
1862, .	5,211	3,967	1,244	4,494	3,139	1,355	9,705	7,106	2,599
1863, .	5,568	3,768	1,797	3,823	2,374	1,449	9,391	6,142	3,246
1864,* .	4,932	3,180	1,752	3,184	1,917	1,267	8,116	5,097	3,019

* Since March 1st.

This increase in female criminality is startling, and not wholly intelligible. It will be observed that the proportion of females committed to the Houses of Correction has always been much greater than of those committed to jails. In 1854 they were but about one in seven of those in Jails, while they were more than one in five of those in Houses of Correction. In 1859 they came nearer to an equal proportion in these two classes of prisons; being a little less than one in five in the jails and a little more than one in five in the Houses of Correction. In 1863 they were a little less than one in three in the jails and considerably more than one in three in the Houses of Correction.

For the present year they have been considerably more than one in three of those committed to Jails ; and almost one-half of those committed to Houses of Correction.

Undoubtedly much of this apparent increase is only relative ; the number of male prisoners having pretty steadily decreased since 1854. But the actual number of female commitments is greater this year and the two preceding ones, than for any other three consecutive years since 1853, and in some counties is very much greater. If we had the means of comparing the workhouse returns with these we should find the increase still more considerable.

The proportion of minors to adults among the prisoners has also increased considerably, but, perhaps, no more than might be expected from the fact that the war has drawn off so many of the adult proportion.

There is one fact, however, not appearing in the statistics, which deserves to be considered by the Legislature and people of Massachusetts. I have learned by my visits to the prisons in the past year, that a great number of these minors are the children, or the brothers and sisters, of soldiers in our army. The boy of six years old, already mentioned as imprisoned for thirty days at Plymouth, was the son of a Massachusetts cavalry soldier, who shortly before his son's imprisonment was killed in General Grant's May campaign against Richmond ; and I have talked with many boys in Jails and Houses of Correction, who were either the sons or the brothers of soldiers or sailors in the service. It may not be extravagant to say that one in four of the many children committed to our prisons have near relatives in the army. The same is true of the female prisoners, though probably not in the same proportion. It has been again and again said to me by prison officers that the mothers, wives, sisters and daughters of soldiers are among the numerous additions to the list of female criminals in the past few years ; and many of these officers ascribe the increase in female crime to the distribution of State Aid and bounty money. The possession of more money than usual makes these poor women idle, and as I have said, exposes them to temptation; they drink, and from this they are led on to worse offences ; while the absence of their sons, husbands and fathers leaves them without restraint or protection.

This is a consequence of the war which we ought to consider; and it should lead us to do what we ought earlier to have done, — establish separate prisons for women and for boys; so that, if we cannot prevent this pitiable increase in crime, we may at least do something to check it, and to reform the offenders. A separate prison for females, placed under the charge of female officers entirely, and visited frequently by those benevolent ladies whose movement in behalf of female convicts I have mentioned, would promise more for the reformation of this class than any method that could be devised. A similar separate prison for boys, in a rural town, say Greenfield, for example, could be made to approach the beneficent character of a Reform School. In it the boys might be instructed in books and in useful labor, and they might be sent forth from it, not as they now go out from our prisons, hardened and made worse, but really reformed. I would have this prison small, because the number who ought to be sent to it would be small. Many of the boys now committed to Jail or to the House of Correction ought rather to go to one of the Reform Schools, and would do so, if these were not constantly full. Provision should be made for them in local Reformatories, which ought to be established in every county, and in all our large cities; the State, if necessary, paying a part of the cost of these establishments. And to facilitate the opening of such Reformatories, as well as to save Massachusetts from the disgrace of treating as criminals so many young children, I would urge on the General Court the importance of fixing by statute the age at which a child shall be deemed capable of committing a crime. By the common law, I am told, seven years is the limit of age, under which no child shall be deemed *capax doli*, or capable of crime. But Edward Livingston, in his proposed code for Louisiana, fixed this limit at nine years, and between that age and fifteen years, it was to be left to the Jury whether the child was really of sufficient discretion to commit the *crime* in question. Let me quote here the words of this noble-hearted legislator, writing forty years ago:

"The provisions of the law have heretofore denounced the same punishment against the first offence of a child, that they awarded to the veteran in guilt; the seducer to crime, and the artless victim of his corruption, were confounded in the same penalty, and that penalty, until lately, was here, and in the land from whence we derive our jurisprudence still is — death. We have substituted imprisonment; but our laws make no other distinction between adults and children, than that contained in the common law, by which all above a certain age, and that a very tender one, are supposed to have sufficient discretion to know both the law and its penalty; and as to those who have not attained that age, it is a matter of inquiry to be determined by evidence, and an instance is recorded, in which an infant of nine years was convicted and executed for murder. For the minor offences, affecting property, indictments against children are frequent; and humanity is equally shocked, whether they are convicted, or, by the lenity of the jury, discharged, to complete their education of infamy. In the penal code which you have under consideration, some material changes are introduced on this subject; an age is fixed, below which guilt cannot be supposed, and the inquiry as to discretion can only take place when the accused is above that age, but below another, at which sufficient capacity may always be presumed. It also contains other provisions, which govern the case in which a child does the prohibited act, in the presence, or under the influence of a parent or superior. But, with all these modifications, nothing materially good under this head would be effected, if, after conviction, the same discipline were indiscriminately applied to children and adults. The necessity of a different course, whether for punishment, or education, or reform, is so clearly pointed out by nature, that he must be an inattentive observer of her laws, who does not perceive it; and it should be considered, that, when a child of tender age commits an offence against the law of society, he acts, for the most part, in obedience to one which with him has a paramount force — that of nature — who has given him strong desires to possess, an ardent passion for novelty, and a free spirit, that with difficulty submits to restraint; while she has withheld that discretion which alone can give a voluntary control over those passions. For acts committed before this discretion is acquired, or when by the visitation of Providence, it is taken away, it is unjust to punish, although the good of society requires that we should restrain."

The restraint provided in the Louisiana Code, in accordance with these views, was in a separate prison for children called *The School of Reform*, to which were to be committed all offenders under the age of eighteen years. To a certain extent our Reform Schools carry out the idea of Livingston, and in some respects they go beyond his plans; but we still lack a *prison* for young offenders, which shall receive those whom the

Reform Schools cannot receive. To send these to an ordinary penitentiary is a cruel absurdity which Livingston has well denounced in a pithy comparison:

"Vice is more infectious than disease; many maladies of the body are not communicated even by contact, but there is no vice that effects the mind, which is not imparted by constant association; and it would be more reasonable to put a man in a pest-house, to cure him of a headache, than to confine a young offender in a penitentiary, organized on the ordinary plan, in order to effect his reformation."

In brief, then, the three remedies to be applied to the increasing criminality among women and children, so far as our prisons are concerned, would be;

I. To forbid the conviction of children under the age of ten years, for any alleged crime.

II. To provide a special prison for boys above the age of ten, to which no adult criminals should be sent.

III. To provide separate prisons for female offenders, with means for classification, instruction and labor, under the exclusive control of female officers.

XIV. THE NATIVITY, TEMPERANCE, ETC., OF OUR PRISONERS.

Before entering upon the details of crime for the year 1864 in the different prisons, something may be said of the remarkable statistics of our prisons, in respect to the Nativity, Personal Habits, etc., of the persons confined.

For the ten years preceding 1864, out of 56,714 prisoners in the Jails, 35,265, or sixty-two per cent. were of foreign birth, and no doubt ten per cent. more were of foreign parentage. In the Houses of Correction for the same period, out of 49,156 prisoners, 32,862 were of foreign birth — almost exactly two-thirds. During the same period, in the same Houses of Correction, out of 49,367 prisoners, 34,958, or more than seventy per cent. were reported intemperate; and in the Jails, 29,239 out of 81,819 were returned as intemperate; about thirty-six per cent. At the same time 28,198 were committed to these Jails for Drunkenness, or as Common Drunkards, a third part of all the commitments; while the number of such commitments to the Houses of Correction was 23,393, or a little less than half of all committed. In the six years 1858–

1863, 9,314 fine and cost prisoners were discharged from the Houses of Correction, of whom 6,997 were discharged as poor convicts; in the Jails for the same period 15,749 fine and cost prisoners were discharged, of whom 12,396 were poor convicts. It thus appears that out of upwards of 25,000 persons sentenced to pay fine and costs, less than 6,000, or about a fourth part, actually paid their fines either by themselves or through friends. The great majority of these were probably persons sentenced for drunkenness. During the year ending October 1, 1864, the proportion of those who paid their fines was larger; the whole number being 3,876, and the number who paid, 1,076. For the first time we have the amount of fines and costs paid, given in the return; for all the prisons it is $15,627.69; giving an average of $14.52 for each prisoner who paid. But even in 1864 the number discharged without payment of the fine was seventy-two per cent. of the whole number.

I have mentioned together, these apparently disconnected particulars, because there is indeed a close connection between them. The great majority of our prisoners are of foreign birth or parentage; intemperance is the curse of our foreign population, and the mode in which we punish it, and the lesser crimes growing out of it is by a fine. But three-fourths of these fines are never paid, and the offender goes out after an imprisonment of not more than thirty days in most cases, to commit *the same offence again*, and undergo the same punishment. Perhaps a majority of what I have called recommitments are cases of this kind. I have found persons who had been sentenced thirty or forty times; and the number reported since the first of March who have been imprisoned more than six times is 205.

It is plain that in respect to these persons, our laws need modification. Instead of a simple fine, or a short sentence of a month or two, these confirmed criminals should receive sentences of a year or two for the lighter crimes, and from three to seven years for the graver offences. Prison discipline could then be brought to operate upon them, and we should have some chance of reforming them. At any rate, they might be taught useful trades, and their labor might make to the community some recompense for the annoyance of their crimes and the cost of their imprisonment. On this point I would refer the Legislature to the opinions of European authorities of experience; particularly to those of Sir Walter Crofton, the founder of the Irish system, and Mr. M. D. Hill, the Recorder of Birmingham, both of whom I have already quoted.

It is very doubtful whether the imposition of a fine for a single act of drunkenness is wise or just. I am told that where it is paid, in most cases it is by the efforts of some relative of the culprit,—oftentimes a wife, a sister or a daughter—whose scanty earnings are affectionately given to set free a wretched drunkard whose first act is to get committed again. It is also alleged that officers arrest and magistrates commit for the sake of the costs of prosecution. An inquiry into this matter is much to be desired.

XV. Summary of Suggestions.

In closing this portion of this Report, let me briefly recapitulate the modifications which, as I believe, ought to be introduced into our code of penal and prison discipline.

I. Penal Discipline.

(1.) The imprisonment of children under ten years of age should be forbidden by statute; and restraint and instruction in Reformatories be substituted for it.

(2.) The number of offences punished by fines should be diminished, and definite imprisonment for a longer or shorter period be substituted.

(3.) Habitual offenders should receive sentences double or treble those now given.

(4.) Conditional remission of punishment, for good conduct in prison, should be made more important, and regulated by a scale of marks similar to those used in Ireland.

(5.) There should be a better oversight of discharged convicts.

II. Prison Discipline.

Perhaps the two last named provisions should come under this head, but I wish to confine this strictly to the management of prisons.

(1.) Separate prisons should be established for females, for boys, and for incorrigible offenders.

(2.) The number of our prisons should be reduced for the sake of economy and efficiency, and they should all be placed under the oversight of a single board of Inspectors, or better still, a single Inspector.

(3.) Classification of the prisoners should be made, on moral grounds, and while good conduct should promote a convict, ill conduct should degrade his rank, and detain him longer in prison.

(4.) Labor in our prisons should be systematized, and the convicts should be allowed a slight interest in its profits.

(5.) Instruction should be made much more thorough, and the office of chaplain more important.

(6.) The prison fare should be reduced to the lowest point consistent with health, not so much for economy, as to allow room for additional rewards to sincere penitence and good behavior.

(7.) The prison officers should be selected with reference to the reformation of the prisoners, and all who have forgotten, or have never learned, that human nature within and without a prison is essentially the same, that reformation is always possible, and that the mercy of God is not suspended by a sentence of the court, should at once be discharged. If our prisons were consolidated it would be unnecessary to fill their places, for they are not very numerous.

In carrying out these changes in our system, should the General Court decide to make them, much time would be necessary, and the experience of other countries, particularly that of Ireland, might be studied with advantage. In recommending them I will not use my own feeble arguments, but turn again to the mature wisdom and the felicitous language of Edward Livingston:

" Let it not be said that this is a theory too refined to be adapted to depraved and degraded convicts. Convicts are men. The most depraved and degraded are men : their minds are moved by the same springs that give activity to those of others; they avoid pain with the same care, and pursue pleasure with the same avidity, that actuate their fellow mortals. It is the false direction only of these great motives that produces the criminal actions which they prompt. To turn them into a course that will promote the true happiness of the individual, by making him cease to injure that of society, should be the great object of penal jurisprudence. The error, it appears to me, lies in considering them as beings of a nature so inferior as to be incapable of elevation, and so bad as to make any amelioration impossible; but crime is the effect principally of intemperance, idleness, ignorance, vicious associations, irreligion and poverty—not of any defective natural organization; and the laws which permit the unrestrained and continual exercise of these causes are themselves the sources of those excesses which legislators, to cover their own inattention, or indolence, or ignorance, impiously and falsely ascribe to the Supreme Being, as if he had created man incapable of receiving the impressions of good. Let us try the experiment before we pronounce that even the degraded convict cannot be reclaimed. It has never yet been tried. Every plan hitherto offered, is manifestly defective, because none has contemplated a complete system, and partial remedies never can succeed.

"But, to think that the best plan which human sagacity could devise will produce reformation in every case, that there will not be numerous exceptions to its general effect, would be to indulge the visionary belief of a moral panacea, applicable to all vices and all crimes; and although this would be quackery in legislation, as absurd as any that has appeared in medicine, yet, to say that there are no general rules by which reformation of the mind may be produced, is as great and fatal an error as to assert that there are in the healing art no useful rules for preserving the general health and bodily vigor of the patient."

These judicious statements were made forty years ago, in a community cursed with slavery, and hampered by anomalous laws and customs. The theory which they uphold has been tried and tested in the penal colonies of Australasia, in Spain and in Ireland, three regions entirely distinct, and among the last in which we should look to see it successfully carried out. What Colonel Montesinos did among the turbulent populace of Spain, Captain Maconochie in the desperate gangs of Norfolk Island, and Sir Walter Crofton amid the ignorance, the misery and the religious dissensions of Ireland, can surely be accomplished in Massachusetts. The mass of the people here would hail a system which combined justice, benevolence and common sense, and it would receive, I am sure, a support which has never been awarded elsewhere, and which would guarantee the most beneficial consequences.

PART THIRD.

PRISON STATISTICS OF MASSACHUSETTS FOR 1864.

In my Annual Report I have given the expenses, the average number, and the approximate whole number of Prisoners in the County Prisons for the year ending September 30, 1864. Some of these particulars I shall here repeat, and also add the details furnished me by returns under the new law, not only from these prisons, but from the State Prison and the Houses of Industry and Reformation for the city of Boston.

First of all I will give the returns respecting the more general facts in the case of the County Prisons.

In the table which follows I have entered the date and cost of these prisons so far as I could ascertain them. The total cost of all must must be at least double what is here given; say two and a quarter millions of dollars.

The whole number of Prisoners includes those in confinement October 1, 1863, and contains some three or four hundred that are counted twice. Probably the true whole number is but little above nine thousand. The commitments will be given elsewhere, with a classification of the sexes. It will be noticed that the number in prison has steadily diminished since October 1, 1863. It is now, (February, 1865,) still smaller than on the 1st of October, 1864, and probably does not exceed one thousand.

TABLE IX.—COUNTY PRISONS, 1864.

Showing the Date, Cost, Capacity and Number of Prisoners of the Jails and Houses of Correction, for the year ending September 30, 1864, together with other Statistics.

COUNTIES, &c.	When built.	Cost.	Number of rooms for Prisoners.	Whole number of Prisoners.	Average number.	No. October 1st, 1863.	No. March 1st, 1864.	No. October 1st, 1864.	No. of Prisoners Vaccinated.	No. com'ted for non-payment of Fines and Costs.	Num'r who paid Fines and Costs.	Amount received for Fines and Costs.
Barnstable County.												
Barnstable Jail,	1821	$14,000 00	—	20	1.73⅝	1	2	4	} = {	8	4	$59 00
" House of Correction,		—	6	16	2.24⅝	2	2	5				
Berkshire County.												
Lenox Jail,	*	—	—	51	4.40	4	1	6	} 140 {	30	12	158 96
" House of Correction,		—	78	117	22.32	21	34	20				
Bristol County.												
New Bedford Jail,	1829	30,000 00	14	105	8	3	7	1	—	190	53	655 00
" House of Correction,	†	4,500 00	160	499	91	95	120	89	a 19	75	40	278 98
Taunton Jail,	1819‡		30	140	8.8	10	12	5				
Dukes County.												
Edgartown Jail,	1824	—	4	2	1	—	1	1	—	—	—	—
" House of Correction,		—	—	—	—	1	—	—	—	—	—	—
Essex County.												
Lawrence Jail,	1853-4	140,000 00	.1	125	8⅝	5	7	12	—	1	1	9 05
" House of Correction,		—	64	314	63.6	60	58	75	—	114	45	527 15

Newburyport Jail,	1825	*	8	78	6.25	1	2	6	—	32	31	$312 17
Ipswich House of Correction,	—	—	94	282	58	49	68	48	25	40	7	121 10
Salem Jail, . . .	1813	*	20	334	15.92	17	20	16	—	87	45	459 66
Franklin County.												
Greenfield Jail, . .	1856-7	$32,500 00	—	15	18	3	—	1	=	1	1	20 00
" House of Correction,	—	—	32	23	38	7	1	3	2	6	4	82 20
Hampden County.												
Springfield Jail, . .	b	40,000 00	—	79	9.25	7	6	14	45	184	36	456 52
" House of Correction,	—	—	194	333	45.5	58	34	48				
Hampshire County.												
Northampton Jail, . .	1852	58,000 00	—	60	3.59	8	1	2	10	46	31	321 93
" House of Correction,	c	—	100	101	8.21	18	8	10				
Middlesex County.												
Cambridge Jail, . .	*	*	10	209	11.17	13	12	22	22	219	117	1,658 56
" House of Correction,	*	*	346	757	144.60	153	150	134	—	3	3	24 45
Concord Jail, . .	1789	—	8	25	2.41	6	2	1	—	50	6	45 80
Lowell Jail, . .	1856	150,000 00	70	180	21	26	16	19				
Nantucket County.												
Nantucket Jail and House of Cor.,	1854	750 00	8	8	2	5	3	1	—	—	—	—
Norfolk County.												
Dedham Jail, . .	1850-1	100,000 00	—	168	14.25	23	12	16	—	72	37	896 96
" House of Correction,	—	—	112	346	61	78	63	50	54d	88	19	365 12

* Unknown.   † Old, 1835; New, 1858.   ‡ Additions, 1861.   § Approximate.   ‖ No return.

a No account kept.   *b* Built at different times.   *c* One wing of jail.   *d* Including jail.

TABLE IX.—Concluded.

COUNTIES, &c.	When built.	Cost	Number of rooms for Prisoners.	Whole number of Prisoners.	Average number.	No. October 1st, 1863.	No. March 1st, 1864.	No. October 1st, 1864.	No. of Prisoners Vaccinated.	No. com'ted for non-payment of Fines and Costs.	Num'r who paid Fines and Costs.	Amount received for Fines and Costs.
Plymouth County.												
Plymouth Jail,	1820	$7,000 00	—	30	—	2	1	5	‡	3	2	—
" House of Correction,	1852	18,700 00	32	46	15	17	11	8	—	15	6	$403 78
Suffolk County.												
Boston Jail,	1851	446,591 47	220	3,489	155†	127	163	157	739	2,267	491	7,741 51
South Boston House of Correction,	1832	—	500	804	235	332	224	203	200	36	—	—
Worcester County.												
Fitchburg Jail,	1858	80,000 00	—	48	4.27	8	2	6	—	—	16	134 44
" House of Correction,			76	113	25.78	29	24	24	120	27	2	—
Worcester Jail,	1819*	—	40	140	8.16	6	7	10	—	3	67	895 35
" House of Correction,		—	85	535	71.99	69	75	52	—	279	—	—
Totals,	—	$1,122,041 47	2,311	9,592	1,133.47	1,264	1,149	1,074	1,376	3,876	1,076	$15,627 69

* Additions, 1836, 1847, 1852.   † Approximate.   ‡ No return.   § Including jail.

The next table shows the whole number of persons committed, and of commitments, in the different county prisons during the year ending September 30, 1864. As these lists are made up partly from my own registers, and partly from those kept at the prisons before mine began, they are more open to mistakes than they otherwise would be ; but they probably show very nearly the state of the case, and are certainly more accurate than the tables of preceding years. I have not extended the classification beyond that of sex, because to complete it would too much delay this Report. The difference between the number of commitments and of persons committed will be seen at once, but it is really much greater than is here given. By comparing the Prison Registers at New Bedford and Taunton for the period between October 1, 1863, and March 1, 1864, I found that one hundred and seventy-two persons were represented by two hundred and fifty-four commitments, in the short space of five months. Probably so great a percentage of reduction could not be made in the commitments for the whole State, but they would be very much reduced by a comparison of all the different Registers. This leads me to believe that the high numbers returned in former years would be lessened considerably if we could learn exactly how many *persons* had been imprisoned in those years. A perfect statistical report would exhibit both the number of persons and the number of commitments, (excluding different commitments for the same crime ;) and in reckoning up the discharges, they should be found to agree with the commitments rather than with the number of persons, since one person committed for five different crimes, or at as many different times, might be discharged in five different ways.

12

TABLE X.

Commitments to the County Prisons, from October 1, 1863, to September 30, 1864.

PRISONS.	JAILS.				HOUSES OF CORRECTION.				Aggregate of Males.	Aggregate of Females.	Aggregate of Persons.	Aggregate of Commitments.
	Males committed.	Females committed.	Total.	Total commitments.	Males committed.	Females committed.	Total.	Total commitments.				
Barnstable,	13	1	14	14	9	1	10	11	22	2	24	25
Lenox,	34	13	47	60	59	37	96	104	93	50	143	164
New Bedford,	32	20	102*	119	251	153	404	433	283	173	506*	552
Taunton,	101	29	130	147	–	–	–	–	101	29	130	147
Edgartown,	2	–	2	2	–	–	–	–	2	–	2	2
Ipswich,	–	–	–	–	72	48	233†	246	72	48	233	246
Lawrence,	107	13	120	129	136	118	254	257	243	131	374	386
Newburyport,	63	14	77	78	–	–	–	–	63	14	77	78
Salem,	269	48	317	330	–	–	–	–	269	48	317	330
Greenfield,	10	2	12	12	–	5	16	16	21	7	28	28

[1865.] SENATE—No. 74. 91

Springfield,	66	13	79	100	172	103	275	291	238	116	354	391
Northampton,	32	20	52	57	64	19	83	92	96	39	135	149
Cambridge,	167	29	196	221	367	237	604	625	534	266	800	846
Concord,	16	3	19	19	—	—	—	—	16	3	19	19
Lowell,	81	73	154	158	—	—	—	—	81	73	154	158
Nantucket,	—	—	2‡	2	1	2	3	3	1	2	5	5
Dedham,	124	21	145	169	137	131	268	274	261	152	413	443
Plymouth,	23	5	28	28	18	11	29	31	41	16	57	59
Boston,	1,900	1,413	3,361§	3,590	222	250	472	491	2,122	1,663	3,833	4,081
Fitchburg,	31	9	40	40	56	28	84	87	87	37	124	127
Worcester,	109	25	134	134	342	124	466	472	451	149	600	606
Totals,	3,180	1,751	5,031	5,409	1,917	1,267	3,297	3,433	5,097	3,018	8,328	8,842

* 50 not classified.   † 113 not classified.   ‡ Not classified.   § 48 not classified.

This is the smallest number of persons committed since 1857, when the returns first began to show the number committed, and also the smallest number of commitments on record. In the year 1862, however, the commitments to the Jails only amounted to 5,211, while this year they are 5,409. The number of *persons* committed to Jail in 1862 was therefore, probably below 5,000. The total for both Jails and Houses of Correction, committed in 1864, is 8,328, but when the persons twice counted are deducted the true number will be below 8,000.

The proportion of minors to adults among these commitments is this year unusually large, (though not shown in this table,) and this is especially true of the commitments of children under fifteen. I have been informed at Newburyport, at Springfield and at several other prisons, that the number of juvenile offenders has never before been so large at those prisons as this year.

The next table will give some information on this point.

Table XI. exhibits the number of different persons who have been in prison in the different prisons mentioned, from the time when the returns under the new registry law began, until October 1, 1864. For the State Prison and the County Prisons, this period is seven months,— that is, from March to October; for the Houses of Industry and Reformation it is four months. In all, however, it includes many who were committed before March 1st, and who were then in prison. At the end of the Table the number of different commitments for these persons is given. The number of persons is considerably less than that of commitments because many persons have been twice and three times committed, and some more than that.

The number of different persons here given is doubtless too great, because any error in searching the registers for duplicate names would be likely to be on that side. If a person for instance had been committed twice in the same prison, he would appear in this table as one person, but if he were committed twice in different prisons, still more, if in different counties, the coincidence of names might not be discovered. Under the old form of questions this sort of error was much more likely to happen than now, but all registers are liable to it, and the more so, the more names they contain.

The classification of these different persons is made in part according to the form in use in previous years. I have added and inserted however, many new particulars, and some of these are important. The classification of recommitted persons, for instance, shows that nearly as many females as males have been previously imprisoned, though the proportion of females to the whole number of prisoners is but about two-fifths. It appears also that the number of females who have been in prison three times and upwards is actually greater than that of males.

Attention is also particularly directed to the number who have been in the army or navy, and in Reform Schools, and those whose parents were convicts.

Annexed to Table XI. are Tables of Crimes and Discharges in the whole State, and following these are the corresponding Tables for each of the County Prisons by itself, with the aggregate for each county; the aggregate for the State being found in Tables XI., XII., and XIII.

TABLE XI.—*Classification of Prisoners in the State.*

	COUNTY PRISONS.			STATE PRISON.	CITY PRISONS.		Totals for State and City Prisons.	Totals for State.
	Jails.	Houses of Correction.	Totals.		House of Reforma'n.	House of Industry.		
Whole No. in Prison,	3,075	2,653	5,728	433	219	618	1,270	6,998
" of Males,	2,019	1,547	3,566	433	194	180	807	4,373
" of Females,	1,056	1,106	2,162	—	25	438	463	2,625
" of Adults,	2,324	2,178	4,502	339	—	560	899	5,401
" of Minors,	751	475	1,226	94	219	58	371	1,597
" of White,	3,004	2,574	5,578	404	217	607	1,228	6,806
" of Colored,	71	79	150	29	2	11	42	192
" of Natives of this State,	*894	†641	†1,535	165	157	90	412	1,947
" of Natives of other States,	415	356	771	112	19	55	186	957
" of Natives of other Countries,	1,757	1,650	3,407	156	43	473	672	4,079
" who had no Education,	946	1,203	2,149	94	3	321	418	2,567
" who could read and write,	158	154	312	2	—	—	2	314
" who had a Common School Education,	‖1,924	§1,270	**3,194	299	210	297	806	4,000
" who had a Superior Education,	15	22	37	38	†	—	†38	75
" who were Married,	1,643	1,608	3,251	178	—	349	527	3,778
" who were Intemperate,	1,715	1,965	3,680	361	—	—	361	4,041
" who had Property to the Value of $1,000,	137	265	402	104	—	—	104	402
" who had been in the Army or Navy,	401	321	722	104	—	—	104	826
" who had been in the Reform School,	42	30	72	—	—	—	—	72
" whose Parents were both Americans,	705	615	1,320	193	5	81	279	1,599
" whose Parents were both Temperate,	2,547	2,096	4,643	327	—	—	327	4,970
" whose Parents were both or either Convicts,	86	118	204	45	—	—	45	249
" of Males committed once before,	390	392	782	38	—	27	65	847
" of Females, " "	215	286	501	—	—	69	69	570

Whole No. of Males committed twice before,	134	179	313	11	—	25	349
" of Females " " "	119	171	290	—	—	54	344
" of Males committed three times before,	60	94	154	5	—	19	178
" of Females " " "	91	93	184	—	—	45	229
" of Males committed four times before,	29	54	83	—	—	12	95
" of Females " " "	55	60	115	1	—	38	153
" of Males committed five times before,	21	49	70	—	—	11	82
" of Females " " "	17	41	58	—	—	26	84
" of Males committed six times before,	21	29	50	—	—	7	57
" of Females " " "	58	18	76	—	—	22	98
" of Males com'ted more than six times before,	36	73	109	—	—	10	119
" of Females " " " " "	37	59	96	—	—	47	143
Total Number of Males who have been in Prison before,	691	870	1,561	55	—	110	1,726
" of Females, " " " " "	592	728	1,320	—	—	299	1,619
Number of Males committed under Fifteen Years of Age,	251	125	376	—	190	—	566
" of Females, " " " " "	10	3	13	—	19	—	32
Total Number of Commitments,	3,264	2,766	6,030	433	219	625	7,307
" who have been in Prison before,	1,283	1,598	2,881	55	—	409	3,345
" committed under Fifteen Years of Age,	261	128	389	—	209	—	598

* Nine not stated.   † Six not stated.   ‡ Fifteen not stated.   ‖ Thirty-two not stated.

§ Four not stated.   ** Thirty-six not stated.

TABLE XII.—*Classification of Crimes in the State.*

	County Prisons.			City Prisons.			Totals for State and City Prisons.	Totals for State.
	Jails.	Houses of Correction.	Totals.	State Prison.	House of Reforma'n.	House of Industry.		
Number committed for Debt,	16	—	16	—	—	—	—	16
" as Witnesses,	60	—	60	—	—	—	—	60
" for Murder,	31	1	32	14	—	—	14	46
" for Manslaughter,	4	5	9	30	—	—	30	39
" for Setting Fires, or Burning,	37	1	38	23	—	—	23	61
" for Robbery,	34	—	34	40	—	1	41	75
" for Larceny,	726	624	1,350	81	18	18	117	1,467
" for Burglary,	20	—	20	22	—	—	22	42
" for Rape, or attempt,	14	—	14	31	—	—	31	45
" for Adultery,	38	21	59	3	—	—	3	62
" for Lewd Conduct,	11	39	50	—	1	65	66	116
" for Keeping Brothels,	78	42	120	—	—	—	—	120
" for Assault,	370	265	635	25	—	5	30	665

Number committed for Perjury,	1	—	1	—	—	—	—	1
" for Forgery,	8	—	8	10	—	—	10	18
" for having or passing Counterfeit Money,	29	2	31	29	—	—	29	60
" for Drunkenness, including Common Drunkards,	1,149	1,157	2,306	—	—	492	492	2,798
" for Violation of Liquor Law,	131	76	207	—	83	—	107	207
" for Vagrancy,	—	158	158	—	7	24	7	265
" for Breaking and Entering,	4	29	33	—	12	—	13	40
" for Stubbornness,	—	—	—	—	79	1	79	13
" for Habitual Truancy,	—	—	—	—	19	—	32	79
" for Idle and Disorderly Conduct,	—	—	—	—	—	13	131	32
" for all other Crimes,	512	336	8,499	125	—	6	1,277	980
" for Crimes of all kinds, excluding debtors and witnesses,	3,197	2,756	5,953	433	219	625	—	7,230
" to Jails on Sentence,	276	—	—	—	—	—	—	—
" for Trial or Examination,	2,921	—	—	—	—	—	—	—

TABLE XIII.—*Classification of Discharges for the State.*

	COUNTY PRISONS.			STATE PRISON.	CITY PRISONS.		Totals for State and City Prisons.	Totals for State.
	Jails.	Houses of Correction.	Totals.		House of Reforma'n.	House of Industry.		
Number discharged by Writ of Habeas Corpus,	3	—	3	—	—	—	—	3
" recognizing or giving Bail,	402	—	402	—	—	—	—	402
" discharged on Expiration of Sentence,	145	1,161	1,306	52	12	260	324	1,630
" discharged by Payment of Fine and Costs,	426	259	685	—	—	—	—	685
" discharged as Poor Convicts,	77	256	333	—	—	—	—	333
" Pardoned,	9	69	78	17	9	28	54	132
" Executed,	—	—	—	—	—	—	—	—
" sent to State Prison,	30	—	30	—	—	—	—	30
" sent to Houses of Correction,	140	—	140	—	—	—	—	140
" sent to Reform School,	12	—	12	—	—	—	—	12
" sent to Nautical Branch,	31	—	31	—	—	—	—	31
" sent to Court and not returned,	379	—	379	—	—	—	—	379
" Escaped and not retaken,	4	7	11	—	—	—	—	11
" of Witnesses discharged,	18	—	18	—	—	—	—	18
" discharged by Order of Overseers,	—	70	70	—	—	—	—	70
" discharged by Police Courts,	908	—	908	—	—	—	—	908
" discharged for Insanity,	—	5	5	—	—	1	1	6

Number discharged for Sickness,	—	—	—	—	—	—	—	12
" that died,	1	6	7	3	—	2	5	72
" transferred to other Jails,	72	—	72	—	—	—	—	6
" of Debtors discharged by Payment of Debt,	6	—	6	—	—	—	—	3
" of Debtors discharged by Order of Creditors,	3	—	3	—	—	—	—	4
" of Debtors discharged by taking Poor Debtor's Oath,	4	—	4	—	—	—	—	421
" discharged by processes not given above,	278	121	399	—	5	17	22	5,308
Whole Number of Discharges reported,	2,948	1,954	4,902	72	26	308	406	5,054
Number of Persons discharged,	2,770	1,883	4,653	72	26	303	401	1,944
" of Persons remaining in Confinement Oct. 1, 1864,	305	770	1,075	361	193	315	869	1,944

TABLE XIV.—*Classification of Prisoners in the County Prisons.*

	Barnstable			Berkshire			Bristol				Dukes			Essex					
	Jail at Barnstable	House of Correction, Barnstable	Aggregates	Jail at Lenox	House of Correction, Lenox	Aggregates	Jail at Taunton	Jail at New Bedford	House of Correction, New Bedford	Aggregates	Jail at Edgartown	House of Correction, Edgartown	Aggregates	Jail at Lawrence	Jail at Newburyport	Jail at Salem	House of Correction, Lawrence	House of Correction, Ipswich	Aggregates
Whole Number in Prison,	14	10	24	25	82	107	83	60	317	460	2	—	2	69	65	162	209	188	693
Males,	13	9	22	18	47	65	63	40	193	296	2	—	2	59	54	136	108	114	471
Females,	1	1	2	7	35	42	20	20	124	164	—	—	—	10	11	26	101	74	222
Adults,	10	10	20	18	61	79	67	47	278	392	2	—	2	37	46	118	163	156	520
Minors,	4	—	4	7	21	28	16	13	39	68	—	—	—	32	19	44	46	32	173
White,	12	9	21	20	68	88	82	54	298	434	2	—	2	69	65	157	206	185	682
Colored,	2	1	3	5	14	19	1	6	19	26	—	—	—	—	—	5	3	3	11
Natives of this State,	14	7	21	13	34	47	31	23	80	134	2	—	2	22	47	63	44	59	235
Natives of other States,	—	—	—	6	16	22	14	11	65	90	—	—	—	15	3	22	24	24	88
Natives of other Countries,	—	3	3	6	32	38	38	26	172	236	—	—	—	32	*14	77	141	105	369
Have had no Education,	—	3	3	4	28	32	35	27	147	209	*	—	—	24	7	23	90	63	207
Could read and write,	14	—	—	—	—	—	7	6	34	47	—	—	—	—	46	24	—	—	70
Have had a Common School Educa'n,	—	7	21	19	51	70	39	26	134	199	1	—	1	45	9	115	118	122	409
Have had a Superior Education,	—	—	—	2	3	5	2	1	2	5	—	—	—	—	‡	—	*	3	3
Were Married,	11	7	7	15	43	58	44	44	210	297	1	—	1	29	33	79	135	122	398
Were Intemperate,	—	9	20	18	67	85	63	37	247	347	1	—	1	24	30	46	128	146	374
Had Property to the Value of $1,000,	1	3	3	2	5	7	4	7	25	35	—	—	1	3	—	2	6	1	12
Had been in the Army or Navy,	—	—	1	6	3	9	13	15	36	64	—	—	—	8	4	24	15	30	81
Had been in the Reform School,	1	—	—	—	—	—	3	1	1	5	—	—	—	—	—	1	—	3	4
Whose Parents were both Americans,	10	5	15	17	39	56	40	25	106	171	1	—	1	21	34	50	29	70	204
Whose Parents were both Temperate,	10	9	19	18	47	65	55	47	246	348	—	—	—	59	29	39	143	130	400

	Whose Parents were both or either Convicts	Males committed once before	Females " " "	Males committed twice before	Females " " "	Males committed three times before	Females " " "	Males committed four times before	Females " " "	Males committed five times before	Females " " "	Males committed six times before	Females " " "	Males com'd more than six times before	Females " " "	Total No. of Males in prison before	" " of Females " "	Males com'ted under Fifteen Yrs. Age	Females " " "	Total Number of Commitments	Total Number who have been in prison before	Total Number committed under Fifteen Years of Age
	25	80	23	42	38	8	11	11	7	6	8	5	7	16	10	168	104	71	1	734	272	72
	6	20	4	15	11	4	4	7	3	5	6	5	5	14	8	70	41	15	–	199	111	15
	8	29	18	12	21	2	4	–	3	1	2	–	1	–	2	44	51	13	1	213	95	14
	8	19	–	10	4	–	3	3	1	–	–	–	1	2	–	34	9	20	–	178	43	20
	3	2	–	–	1	1	–	–	–	–	–	–	–	–	–	3	1	6	–	66	4	6
	–	10	1	5	1	1	–	1	–	–	–	–	–	–	–	17	2	17	–	78	19	17
	–	–	–	–	–	–	–	–	–	–	–	–	–	–	–	2	–	–				
	–	–	–	–	–	–	–	–	–	–	–	–	–	–	–	–	–	–				
	–	–	–	–	–	–	–	–	–	–	–	–	–	–	–	2	–	–				
	23	51	36	43	18	18	21	11	19	10	5	6	3	34	17	173	119	24	–	507	292	24
	12	34	28	32	18	15	17	8	16	8	5	2	2	23	13	122	99	15		334	221	15
	6	4	4	8	–	1	2	2	1	1	–	1	1	4	3	21	11	5	–	77	32	5
	5	13	4	3	–	2	2	1	2	1	–	3	–	7	1	30	9	4	–	96	39	4
	–	10	9	10	2	4	1	3	1	2	–	1	–	1	2	22	15	3	1	123	37	4
	7	7	9	2	1	2	–	3	1	2	–	1	–	1	2	18	13	2	–	87	31	2
	3	2	1	–	–	2	1	–	–	–	–	–	–	–	–	4	2	1	–	36	6	2
	–	2	–	2	–	2	–	–	–	–	–	–	–	–	2	–	8	–	2	25	8	2
	–	–	–	–	–	–	–	–	–	–	–	–	–	2	–	2	–	–		11	2	–
	–	2	–	2	–	2	–	–	–	–	–	–	–	–	6	–	2	–	14	6	2	

* One not stated.   ‡ Three not stated.   ¶ No prisoners returned.

102 PRISONS AND PRISON DISCIPLINE. [Mar.

TABLE XIV.—*Classification of Prisoners in the County Prisons*—Continued.

	FRANKLIN.			HAMPDEN.			HAMPSHIRE.			MIDDLESEX.					NANTUCKET.		
	Jail at Greenfield.	House of Correction, Greenfield.	Aggregates.	Jail at Springfield.	House of Correction, Springfield.	Aggregates.	Jail at Northampton.	House of Correction, Northampton.	Aggregates.	Jail at Cambridge.	Jail at Concord.	Jail at Lowell.	House of Correction, Cambridge.	Aggregates.	Jail at Nantucket.	House of Correction, Nantucket.	Aggregates.
Whole Number in Prison,	12	14	26	58	205	263	26	46	72	131	14	95	478	718	—	3	3
Males,	10	9	19	53	134	187	13	35	48	111	11	47	283	452	—	1	1
Females,	2	5	7	5	71	76	13	11	24	20	3	48	195	266	—	2	2
Adults,	9	11	20	35	168	203	23	37	60	93	9	76	402	580	—	3	3
Minors,	3	3	6	23	37	60	3	9	12	38	5	19	76	138	—	—	—
White,	11	14	25	56	196	252	26	45	71	127	14	95	475	711	—	2	2
Colored,	1	—	1	2	9	11	—	—	1	4	—	—	3	7	—	1	1
Natives of this State,	5	7	12	17	41	58	7	18	25	34	8	18	92	152	—	2	2
Natives of other States,	3	3	6	11	32	43	1	*4	5	*23	2	20	*42	87	—	—	—
Natives of other Countries,	†2	4	6	30	132	162	18	23	41	73	4	57	343	477	—	2	2
Have had no Education,	3	5	8	20	90	110	12	18	30	44	1	51	269	365	—	3	3
Could read and write,	1	1	2	23	69	92	14	27	41	86	2	44	208	340	—	—	—
Have had a Common School Educa'n,	6	8	14	15	42	57	—	*	—	1	—	—	1	2	—	—	—
Have had a Superior Education,	—	—	—	—	4	4	—	—	—	—	—	—	—	—	—	—	—
Were Married,	5	9	14	21	76	97	21	29	50	68	6	63	325	462	—	2	2
Were Intemperate,	5	9	14	43	171	214	18	37	55	67	7	79	359	512	—	3	3
Had Property to the Value of $1,000,	—	—	—	3	11	14	1	1	2	15	1	2	54	72	—	1	1
Had been in the Army or Navy,	—	—	—	5	20	25	2	5	7	38	—	12	63	113	—	—	—
Had been in the Reform School,	—	—	—	—	—	1	—	—	—	2	—	6	4	12	—	—	—
Whose Parents were both Americans,	6	11	17	18	46	64	7	20	27	35	3	26	83	147	—	2	2
Whose Parents were both Temperate,	4	4	8	48	141	189	16	30	46	114	3	87	398	602	—	3	3

Whose Parents were both or either Convicts, ...	–	1	1	1	8	9	2	3	5	9	–	6	28	43	–	–	–
Males committed once before, . .	–	1	1	9	20	29	2	7	9	22	–	12	52	86	–	1	1
Females " " " . .	–	–	–	1	8	9	3	2	5	3	–	12	46	61	–	1	1
Males committed twice before, . .	–	–	–	2	9	11	3	6	9	–	–	5	30	35	–	–	–
Females " " " . .	–	–	–	1	5	6	2	3	5	–	–	5	21	26	–	–	–
Males committed three times before,	–	–	–	2	11	13	1	2	3	–	–	2	19	21	–	–	–
Females " " " "	–	–	–	–	6	6	1	–	1	–	–	4	22	26	–	–	–
Males committed four times before, .	–	–	–	–	5	5	–	1	1	–	–	2	12	14	–	–	–
Females " " " "	–	–	–	–	6	6	1	1	2	–	–	4	9	13	–	–	–
Males committed five times before, .	–	–	–	1	4	5	–	3	3	–	–	–	9	9	–	–	–
Females " " " " .	–	–	–	–	7	7	–	–	–	–	–	2	4	6	–	–	–
Males committed six times before, .	–	–	–	–	2	2	1	–	1	–	–	1	7	8	–	–	–
Females " " " " .	–	–	–	–	2	2	–	–	–	–	–	3	2	5	–	–	–
Males com'd more than six times before,	–	–	–	1	4	5	–	–	–	–	–	4	5	9	–	–	–
Females " " " " " "	–	–	–	–	10	10	–	–	–	–	–	4	2	6	–	–	–
Total No. of Males in prison before,	–	1	1	15	55	70	7	19	26	22	–	26	134	182	–	1	1
" " of Females " "	–	–	–	2	44	46	7	6	13	3	–	34	106	143	–	1	1
Males com'ted under Fifteen Yrs. Age,	2	3	5	5	22	27	–	–	–	10	5	2	21	38	–	–	–
Females " " " " "	–	–	–	–	1	1	–	–	–	1	–	–	1	2	–	–	–
Total Number of Commitments, .	12	14	26	79	215	294	28	52	80	150	14	99	494	757	–	3	3
Total Number who have been in prison before, ...	–	1	1	17	99	116	14	25	39	25	–	60	240	325	–	2	2
Total Number committed under Fifteen Years of Age, . . .	2	2	4	5	23	28	–	–	–	11	5	2	22	40	–	–	–

* One not stated.

† Two not stated.

TABLE XIV.—*Classification of Prisoners in the County Prisons—Concluded.*

	NORFOLK.			PLYMOUTH.			SUFFOLK.			WORCESTER.			
	Jail at Dedham.	House of Correction, Dedham.	Aggregates.	Jail at Plymouth.	House of Correction, Plymouth.	Aggregates.	Jail at Boston.	House of Correction, South Boston.	Aggregates.	Jail at Worcester.	Jail at Fitchburg.	House of Correction, Worcester.	House of Correction, Fitchburg.	Aggregates.
Whole Number in Prison,	111	213	324	17	25	42	2,023	474	2,497	80	28	321	68	497
Males,	94	104	198	13	14	27	1,194	215	1,409	67	21	238	43	369
Females,	17	109	126	4	11	15	829	259	1,088	13	7	83	25	128
Adults,	66	187	253	14	21	35	1,575	383	1,958	61	18	262	36	377
Minors,	45	26	71	3	4	7	448	91	539	19	10	59	32	120
White,	109	209	318	17	25	42	1,980	458	2,438	80	28	316	68	492
Colored,	2	4	6	—	—	—	43	16	59	—	—	—	—	5
Natives of this State,	39	41	80	11	12	23	507	107	614	27	7	†70	*27	131
Natives of other States,	18	18	36	2	3	5	244	80	324	12	9	33	12	64
Natives of other Countries,	54	154	208	4	10	14	1,272	287	1,559	41	8	215	28	293
Have had no Education,	40	106	146	3	12	15	615	168	783	29	5	163	40	240
Could read and write,	35	45	80	—	—	—	—	—	—	†	12	—	5	10
Have had a Common School Educa'n,	13	57	70	14	12	26	1,403	305	1,708	47	†3	157	20	236
Have had a Superior Education,	82	5	7	—	*	—	5	*	5	2	6	1	3	6
Were Married,	56	140	196	13	7	20	1,091	277	1,368	41	3	198	27	279
Were Intemperate,	41	167	208	6	7	13	1,170	322	1,492	43	7	266	29	344
Had Property to the Value of $1,000,	7	10	17	2	1	3	76	103	179	11	—	29	4	47
Had been in the Army or Navy,	17	21	38	4	1	5	230	66	296	15	7	50	11	83
Had been in the Reform School,	—	—	—	—	—	—	27	17	44	1	—	4	1	6
Whose Parents were both Americans,	22	29	51	12	11	23	345	82	427	25	7	58	24	114
Whose Parents were both Temperate,	95	192	287	15	9	24	1,826	432	2,258	60	21	264	48	393

	1	2	3	4	5	6	7	8	9	10	11	12	13	14
Whose Parents were both or either Convicts,	8	7	15			1	29	16	45	4	2	12	9	27
Males committed once before,	7	10	17	1	5	6	262	140	402	17	6	55	11	89
Females " "	3	15	18		2	2	180	132	312	2	1	15	6	24
Males committed twice before,	4	14	18		1	1	86	34	120	5	1	21	3	30
Females " "		19	18				105	58	163			10	4	14
Males committed three times before,	1	12	19		1	1	45	10	55			13	4	17
Females " " " "	1	7	13		1	1	77	25	102			6	1	7
Males committed four times before,		6	8				19	3	22		1	6	2	9
Females " " "		5	6		1	1	46	11	57			4	1	5
Males committed five times before,	1	3	5		1	1	17	5	22			8	1	9
Females " " "		4	4				15	11	26			1		1
Males committed six times before,		2	4	1	1	2	14	2	16			5		5
Females " " "		5	2				53	3	56				1	1
Males com'd more than six times before,		2	5		1	1	16	9	25	1	1	9	1	11
Females " " " " "		5	2		9	11	29	14	43	1		5		6
Total No. of Males in prison before,	13	54	67	2	4	4	459	203	662	23	9	117	21	170
" " of Females " "	4	54	58	1	2	2	505	254	759	2	1	41	14	58
Males com'ted under Fifteen Yrs. Age,	27	5	32		1	1	140	2	142	3	1	18	8	30
Females " " " "	1		1				5		5	1		1		2
Total Number of Commitments,	116	216	332	17	25	42	2,094	506	2,600	80	28	326	71	505
Total Number who have been in prison before,	17	108	125	2	13	15	964	457	1,421	25	10	158	35	228
Total Number committed under Fifteen Years of Age,	28	5	33	1	1	2	145	2	147	4	1	19	8	32

* One not stated.　† Two not stated.　‡ Three not stated.　‖ Five not stated.　§ Twenty-one not stated.

TABLE XV.—Classification of Crimes in the County Prisons.

	Barnstable — Jail at Barnstable	Barnstable — House of Correction, Barnstable	Barnstable — Aggregates	Berkshire — Jail at Lenox	Berkshire — House of Correction, Lenox	Berkshire — Aggregates	Bristol — Jail at Taunton	Bristol — Jail at New Bedford	Bristol — House of Correction, New Bedford	Bristol — Aggregates	Dukes — Jail at Edgartown	Dukes — House of Correction, Edgartown	Dukes — Aggregates	Essex — Jail at Lawrence	Essex — Jail at Newburyport	Essex — Jail at Salem	Essex — House of Correction, Lawrence	Essex — House of Correction, Ipswich	Essex — Aggregates
Committed for Debt,	1	—	1	—	—	—	2	—	—	2	—	—	—	2	—	—	—	—	2
" as Witnesses,	—	—	—	—	—	—	—	12	—	12	—	—	—	3	—	2	—	—	5
" for Murder,	—	—	—	—	—	—	—	2	—	2	1	—	1	—	—	1	—	—	1
" for Manslaughter,	—	—	—	1	—	1	—	—	—	—	—	—	—	—	—	—	—	—	—
" for Setting Fires or Burn'g,	—	—	—	1	—	1	—	—	—	—	—	—	—	—	2	1	—	—	3
" for Robbery,	—	—	—	—	—	—	—	1	—	1	—	—	—	3	—	—	—	—	3
" for Larceny,	3	1	4	8	25	33	16	18	43	77	—	—	—	18	1	37	50	43	149
" for Burglary,	1	—	1	2	—	2	3	1	—	4	—	—	—	4	1	4	—	—	9
" for Rape, or attempt,	1	—	1	—	—	—	—	—	—	—	—	—	—	3	—	—	—	—	3
" for Adultery,	—	—	—	2	1	3	1	5	3	9	—	—	—	—	1	1	7	2	11
" for Lewd Conduct,	—	—	—	3	—	3	1	—	—	1	—	—	—	2	—	1	11	4	18

Committed for Keeping Brothels,	—	—	—	—	1	2	2	1	11	14	—	—	—	—	—	1	1	2	4
" for Assault,	4	3	7	8	13	21	8	—	22	30	—	—	—	3	4	12	10	24	53
" for Perjury,	1	—	1	—	—	—	—	—	—	—	—	—	—	—	—	—	—	—	—
" for Forgery,	—	—	—	—	—	—	2	—	—	2	1	—	1	—	—	2	—	—	2
" for making, having or pass'g Counterfeit Money,	—	—	—	1	—	1	—	—	1	1	—	—	—	3	2	2	—	—	7
" for Drunkenness, includ'g Common Drunkards,	—	2	2	—	26	26	55	14	165	234	—	—	—	5	11	47	97	79	239
" for Violating Liquor Law,	—	—	—	—	—	—	1	3	16	20	—	—	—	1	21	25	1	5	53
" for Vagrancy,	—	—	—	—	6	6	—	—	12	12	—	—	—	—	—	—	14	26	40
" for Breaking and Entering,	—	—	—	—	—	—	—	4	3	7	—	—	—	—	—	—	—	—	—
" for all other Crimes,	3	5	8	8	13	21	5	16	54	75	—	—	—	31	25	40	21	14	131
Whole Number of Crimes reported,	13	11	24	35	*85	120	94	65	†330	489	2	—	2	73	68	174	212	‖199	726
Committed to Jails on Sentence,	3	—	22	2	—	2	24	2	—	26	—	—	—	3	2	49	—	—	54
" for Trial or Examination,	10	—	10	33	—	33	70	63	—	133	2	—	2	70	66	125	—	—	261

* One committed for two crimes.   † Two committed for two crimes each.   ‖ Four committed for two crimes each.

TABLE XV.—Classification of Crimes in the County Prisons—Continued.

	Franklin			Hampden			Hampshire			Middlesex					Nantucket		
	Jail at Greenfield	House of Correction, Greenfield	Aggregates	Jail at Springfield	House of Correction, Springfield	Aggregates	Jail at Northampton	House of Correction, Northampton	Aggregates	Jail at Cambridge	Jail at Concord	Jail at Lowell	House of Correction, Cambridge	Aggregates	Jail at Nantucket	House of Correction, Nantucket	Aggregates
Committed for Debt,	1	—	1	—	—	—	—	—	—	8	—	1	—	9	—	—	—
" as Witnesses,	—	—	—	—	—	—	—	—	—	3	—	1	—	4	—	—	—
" for Murder,	—	—	—	12	—	12	—	—	—	1	—	1	—	2	—	—	—
" for Manslaughter,	—	—	—	—	—	—	—	—	—	—	—	1	3	4	—	—	—
" for Setting Fires or Burn'g,	—	—	—	12	—	12	—	—	—	15	1	1	1	18	—	—	—
" for Robbery,	—	—	—	—	—	—	—	—	—	3	—	1	—	4	—	—	—
" for Larceny,	5	3	8	39	44	83	6	7	13	30	6	13	82	131	—	—	—
" for Burglary,	—	—	—	—	—	—	—	—	—	1	—	—	—	1	—	—	—
" for Rape, or attempt,	—	—	—	—	—	—	—	—	—	2	—	—	—	2	—	—	—
" for Adultery,	1	—	1	1	—	1	2	—	2	6	—	7	5	18	—	—	—
" for Lewd Conduct,	1	2	3	—	—	—	—	—	—	—	—	—	3	3	—	—	—

Committed for Keeping Brothels,	–	–	–	–	–	–	–	–	–	–	–	–
" for Assault,	4	7	10	17	1	12	13	24	2	6	58	90
" for Perjury,	–	–	–	–	–	–	–	–	–	–	–	–
" for Forgery,	–	–	–	–	–	–	–	–	–	–	–	–
" for making, having or pass'g Counterfeit Money,	1	1	–	–	–	–	–	–	–	2	–	2
" for Drunkenness, includ'g Common Drunkards,	1	3	4	112	116	9	24	33	9	1	51	246	307
" for Violating Liquor Law,	–	1	1	1	1	1	–	1	10	2	–	21	33
" for Vagrancy,	–	–	–	16	16	–	1	1	–	–	–	41	41
" for Breaking and Entering,	–	–	1	–	1	–	–	1	–	–	–	2	2
" for all other Crimes,	2	1	3	30	34	6	6	12	39	2	14	43	98
Whole Number of Crimes reported,	11	14	25	215	294	28	51	79	†140	14	97	†505	756
Committed to Jails on Sentence,	–	–	–	–	1	17	–	17	20	1	4	–	25
" for Trial or Examination,	11	–	11	–	78	11	–	11	120	13	93	–	226

† Two committed for two crimes each.   ‡ Three committed for two crimes each.

110 PRISONS AND PRISON DISCIPLINE. [Mar.

TABLE XVI.—*Classification of Crimes in the County Prisons—Concluded.*

	NORFOLK.			PLYMOUTH.			SUFFOLK.			WORCESTER.				
	Jail at Dedham.	House of Correction, Dedham.	Aggregates.	Jail at Plymouth.	House of Correction, Plymouth.	Aggregates.	Jail at Boston.	House of Correction, South Boston.	Aggregates.	Jail at Worcester.	Jail at Fitchburg.	House of Correction, Worcester.	House of Correction, Fitchburg.	Aggregates.
Committed for Debt,	1	–	1	–	–	–	–	–	–	–	–	–	–	–
" as Witnesses,	–	–	–	–	–	–	39	–	39	–	–	–	–	–
" for Murder,	1	–	1	–	1	1	10	–	10	2	–	–	–	2
" for Manslaughter,	–	–	–	–	–	–	2	2	4	–	–	–	–	–
" for Setting Fires, or Burn'g,	3	–	3	–	–	–	–	–	–	1	–	–	–	1
" for Robbery,	–	–	–	–	–	–	23	–	23	3	–	–	–	3
" for Larceny,	29	29	58	17	5	22	440	207	647	26	14	61	24	125
" for Burglary,	1	–	1	–	–	–	–	–	–	2	–	–	–	2
" for Rape, or attempt,	1	–	1	4	–	4	6	–	6	–	1	–	–	1
" for Adultery,	1	–	1	–	–	–	2	–	2	3	1	2	1	7
" for Lewd Conduct,	–	8	8	–	–	–	1	3	4	2	–	4	4	10

Committed for Keeping Brothels,	—	—	—	—	—	—	—	70	25	95	—	—	—	—	1	1
" for Assault,	21	14	35	—	2	1	3	250	51	301	16	2	32	11	61	
" for Perjury,	—	—	—	—	—	—	—	—	—	—	—	—	—	—	—	
" for Forgery,	—	—	—	—	—	—	—	2	—	2	1	—	—	—	1	
" for making, having or pass'g Counterfeit Money,	—	—	—	—	—	—	—	15	1	16	—	3	—	—	3	
" for Drunkenness, includ'g Common Drunkards,	9	119	128	—	8	8	8	930	82	1,012	3	—	181	13	197	
" for Violating Liquor Law,	6	4	10	4	—	8	12	50	8	58	6	1	9	2	18	
" for Vagrancy,	—	26	26	—	—	1	—	—	4	4	—	—	12	—	12	
" for Breaking and Entering,	—	3	3	3	—	1	1	—	18	18	—	—	—	—	—	
" for all other Crimes,	42	13	55	30	—	25	4	251	94	345	15	6	26	15	62	
Whole Number of Crimes reported,	114	216	330	1	—	—	55	‡2,052	§495	2,547	80	28	327	71	506	
Committed to Jails on Sentence,	67	—	67	1	—	—	1	70	—	70	—	10	—	—	10	
" for Trial or Examination,	47	—	47	29	—	—	29	1,982	—	1,982	80	18	—	—	98	

‡ Three committed for two crimes each.   § Ten committed for two crimes each.

TABLE XVI.—Classification of Discharges from the County Prisons.

	Barnstable			Berkshire			Bristol				Dukes			Essex					
	Jail at Barnstable	House of Correction, Barnstable	Aggregates	Jail at Lenox	House of Correction, Lenox	Aggregates	Jail at Taunton	Jail at New Bedford	House of Correction, New Bedford	Aggregates	Jail at Edgartown	House of Correction, Edgartown	Aggregates	Jail at Lawrence	Jail at Newburyport	Jail at Salem	House of Correction, Lawrence	House of Correction, Ipswich	Aggregates
Discharged by Writ of Habeas Corpus,	—	—	—	—	—	—	—	—	—	—	—	—	—	—	—	1	—	—	1
Recognizing or Giving Bail,	2	—	2	12	—	12	9	13	—	22	1	—	1	11	17	38	—	—	66
Discharged on Expiration of Sentence,	—	3	3	—	39	39	2	—	139	141	—	—	—	3	2	14	96	118	233
" by Payment of Fine and Costs,	—	—	—	1	7	8	28	—	26	54	—	—	—	—	22	28	25	4	79
" as Poor Convicts,	1	—	1	—	8	8	15	—	63	78	—	—	—	—	4	12	—	—	16
Pardoned,	—	—	—	—	1	1	—	—	7	7	—	—	—	—	—	—	15	5	20
Executed,	—	—	—	—	—	—	—	—	—	—	—	—	—	—	—	—	—	—	—
Sent to State Prison,	1	—	1	—	—	—	—	4	—	4	—	—	—	—	—	—	—	—	1
" to Houses of Correction,	1	—	1	3	—	3	—	8	—	8	—	—	—	—	—	1	—	—	2
" to Reform School,	—	—	—	—	—	—	2	2	—	4	—	—	—	—	—	2	—	—	2
" to Nautical Branch,	—	—	—	—	—	—	2	—	—	2	—	—	—	—	2	2	—	—	4

Row	1	2	3	4	5	6	7	8	9	10	11	12	13	14	15	16	17	18	19
Sent to Court and not returned,	49	—	—	12	—	37	—	—	—	20	—	12	8	—	—	—	—	—	—
Escaped and not retaken,	3	3	—	—	—	—	—	—	—	—	—	—	—	1	1	—	1	—	1
Witnesses discharged,	2	—	—	1	—	1	—	—	—	12	—	12	—	—	—	—	—	—	—
Discharged by Order of Overseers,	12	12	—	—	—	—	—	—	—	4	4	—	—	7	7	—	1	1	—
" by Police Courts,	—	—	—	—	—	—	—	—	—	—	—	—	—	—	—	—	—	—	—
" for Insanity,	—	—	—	—	—	—	—	—	—	—	—	—	—	—	—	—	—	—	—
" for Sickness,	—	—	—	—	—	—	—	—	—	—	—	—	—	—	—	—	—	—	—
Died,	1	1	—	—	—	—	—	—	—	1	1	—	—	—	—	1	—	—	—
Transferred to other Jails,	19	—	—	18	—	—	—	—	—	27	—	23	4	—	—	—	—	—	—
Debtors disch'd by Payment of Debt,	—	—	—	—	—	1	—	—	—	—	—	—	—	1	—	—	1	—	—
" " by Order of Creditors,	2	—	—	—	—	—	—	—	—	—	—	—	—	—	—	1	—	—	—
" " by taking Poor Debtor's Oath,	—	—	—	—	—	2	—	—	—	—	—	—	—	1	—	—	—	—	—
Discharged by processes not given above,	60	3	2	33	11	11	—	—	—	23	1	1	21	13	2	11	5	2	3
Whole Number of Discharges reported,	572	146	138	162	60	66	1	—	1	407	241	75	91	94	65	29	16	6	10
" of Persons discharged,	326	140	124	146	59	57	1	—	1	367	230	59	78	82	62	20	16	6	10
Persons remaining in Confinement,	157	48	75	16	6	12	1	—	1	95	89	1	5	26	20	6	9	5	4

TABLE XVI.—Classification of Discharges from the County Prisons—Continued.

	NANTUCKET			MIDDLESEX					HAMPSHIRE			HAMPDEN			FRANKLIN		
	Jail at Nantucket.	House of Correction, Nantucket.	Aggregates.	Jail at Cambridge.	Jail at Concord.	Jail at Lowell.	House of Correction, Cambridge.	Aggregates.	Jail at Northampton.	House of Correction, Northampton.	Aggregates.	Jail at Springfield.	House of Correction, Springfield.	Aggregates.	Jail at Greenfield.	House of Correction, Greenfield.	Aggregates.
Discharged by Writ of Habeas Corpus,	—	—	—	1	—	—	—	1	—	—	—	—	—	—	—	—	—
Recognizing or Giving Bail,	—	—	—	31	4	10	—	45	5	—	5	16	—	16	5	—	5
Discharged on Expiration of Sentence,	—	1	1	10	2	9	200	221	1	19	20	1	50	51	—	8	8
" by Payment of Fine and Costs,	—	1	1	3	3	6	67	79	1	18	19	—	34	34	1	2	3
" as Poor Convicts,	—	—	—	3	—	—	—	3	—	—	—	—	—	—	—	—	—
Pardoned,	—	—	—	—	—	2	3	5	—	—	—	—	4	4	—	—	—
Executed,	—	—	—	—	—	—	—	—	—	—	—	—	—	—	—	—	—
Sent to State Prison,	—	—	—	1	—	—	—	1	—	—	—	—	—	—	—	—	—
" to Houses of Correction,	—	—	—	1	—	—	—	1	4	—	4	3	—	3	—	—	—
" to Reform School,	—	—	—	5	—	—	—	5	1	—	1	—	—	—	1	—	1
" to Nautical Branch,	—	—	—	—	1	—	—	1	—	—	—	—	—	—	—	—	—

1865.] SENATE—No. 74. 115

Sent to Court and not returned	Escaped and not retaken	Witnesses discharged	Discharged by Order of Overseers	" by Police Courts	" for Insanity	" for Sickness	Died	Transferred to other Jails	Debtors disch'd by Payment of Debt	" by Order of Creditors	" by taking Poor Debtor's Oath	Discharged by processes not given above	Whole Number of Discharges reported	" of Persons discharged	Persons remaining in Confinement
—	—	—	—	—	—	—	—	—	—	—	—	—	2	2	1
—	—	—	—	—	—	—	—	—	—	—	—	—	2	2	1
—	—	—	—	—	—	—	—	—	—	—	—	—	—	—	—
18	3	4	11	—	3	—	—	22	3	—	—	147	572	542	176
—	—	—	11	—	3	—	—	—	—	—	—	69	353	344	134
16	3	1	—	—	—	—	—	1	—	—	—	32	80	76	19
2	—	—	—	—	—	—	—	—	—	—	—	1	13	13	1
—	—	3	—	—	—	—	—	21	3	—	—	45	126	109	22
8	—	—	1	—	—	—	1	—	—	—	—	9	67	60	12
—	—	—	1	—	—	—	—	—	—	—	—	3	41	36	10
8	—	—	—	—	—	—	—	—	—	—	—	6	26	24	2
24	—	—	4	—	—	—	—	—	—	—	1	20	230	201	62
—	—	—	4	—	—	—	—	—	—	—	—	—	165	157	48
24	—	—	—	—	—	—	—	—	—	—	1	20	65	44	14
—	—	—	—	—	—	—	—	—	1	—	—	4	22	22	4
—	—	—	—	—	—	—	—	—	—	—	—	1	11	11	3
—	—	—	—	—	—	—	—	1	—	—	3	11	11	11	1

TABLE XVI.—*Classification of Discharges from the County Prisons—Concluded.*

	NORFOLK.			PLYMOUTH.			SUFFOLK.			WORCESTER.				
	Jail at Dedham.	House of Correction, Dedham.	Aggregates.	Jail at Plymouth.	House of Correction, Plymouth.	Aggregates.	Jail at Boston.	House of Correction, South Boston.	Aggregates.	Jail at Worcester.	Jail at Fitchburg.	House of Correction, Worcester.	House of Correction, Fitchburg.	Aggregates.
Discharged by Writ of Habeas Corpus,	–	–	–	–	–	–	1	–	1	–	–	–	–	–
Recognizing or Giving Bail,	14	–	14	–	–	–	185	–	185	29	–	–	–	29
Discharged on Expiration of Sentence,	12	87	99	–	11	11	87	261	348	2	–	98	31	131
" by Payment of Fine and Costs,	27	10	37	1	–	1	304	1	305	1	–	55	9	65
" as Poor Convicts,	–	–	–	1	4	5	41	–	41	–	–	106	2	108
Pardoned,	–	6	6	–	1	1	7	15	22	–	–	10	2	12
Executed,	–	–	–	–	–	–	–	–	–	–	–	–	–	–
Sent to State Prison,	1	–	1	–	–	–	18	–	18	–	2	–	–	4
" to Houses of Correction,	4	–	4	–	–	1	91	–	91	–	5	–	–	18
" to Reform School,	1	–	1	–	–	–	3	–	3	–	–	–	–	–
" to Nautical Branch,	1	–	1	–	–	–	23	–	23	–	–	–	–	–

Sent to Court and not returned,	27	—	—	12	15	233	—	233	—	—	—	—	—	—
Escaped and not retaken,	1	1	—	—	—	—	—	—	—	—	—	2	2	—
Witnesses discharged,	—	—	—	—	—	—	—	—	—	—	—	—	—	—
Discharged by Order of Overseers,	4	1	3	—	—	—	—	—	1	1	—	25	25	—
" by Police Courts,	—	—	—	—	—	908	—	908	—	—	—	—	—	—
" for Insanity,	2	—	2	—	—	—	—	—	—	—	—	—	—	—
" for Sickness,	—	—	—	—	—	—	—	—	—	—	—	—	—	—
Died,	—	—	—	—	—	—	4	—	—	—	—	1	—	1
Transferred to other Jails,	4	—	—	—	4	4	—	—	—	—	—	1	—	1
Debtors disch'd by Payment of Debt,	—	—	—	—	—	—	—	—	—	—	—	—	—	—
" " by Order of Creditors,	—	—	—	—	—	—	—	—	—	—	—	—	—	—
" " by taking Poor Debtor's Oath,	—	—	—	—	4	2	1	2	—	—	—	—	—	—
Discharged by processes not given above,	8	1	—	3	70	27	282	26	9	—	9	74	36	38
Whole Number of Discharges reported,	413	47	274	22	70	2,211	271	1,929	29	17	12	266	166	100
" of Persons discharged,	405	44	269	22	70	2,137	203	1,866	29	17	12	257	163	95
Persons remaining in Confinement,	92	24	52	6	10	360	203	157	13	8	5	66	50	16

In the foregoing tables some discrepancies will appear. The whole number of crimes is a little smaller than that of commitments; which may be owing to the fact that the same person, for the same crime, has occasionally been entered twice. The discharges as reported do not correspond exactly either to the commitments or to the number of persons in prison, being less than the former and greater than the latter. In neither case, however, is this discrepancy very great; and it will be found that the tables are much more accurate so far as they go, than those in former years, while it is believed that the means exist of making future returns still more precise.

The following table exhibits the cases of sickness and the punishments in the different prisons from which returns have been received, during the period of seven months, for the County Prisons and the State Prison, and four months for the Houses of Industry and Reformation.

It will be seen that neither the sickness nor the punishment, if correctly reported, has been very great; the proportion of sick to the average number being less than two per cent., and of punishments less than half of one per cent. The punishment in use is generally solitary confinement.

NOTE TO TABLE XVI. The whole number of persons remaining in confinement October 1, 1864, in the county prisons, is incorrectly stated on page 88 as 1,074. The true number is 1,075, as found on page 99.

TABLE XVII.—*Sickness and Punishment in State, County, and City Prisons.*

	Number of Sick discharged between March 1 and October 1, 1864.	Number of Days' Sickness.	Number who had been punished once.	Number who had been punished twice.	Number who had been punished three times.	Number who had been punished more than three times.	Whole number who had been punished.	Number of Punishments.
House of Correction, Lenox,	6	27	6	2	1	1	10	19
Jail at New Bedford,	1	3	—	—	—	—	—	—
House of Correction, New Bedford,	11	365	16	2	1	1	20	28
House of Correction, Ipswich,	32	731	12	1	1	—	14	17
House of Correction, Lawrence,	28	180	20	6	2	5	33	66
Jail at Newburyport,	1	20	—	—	—	—	—	—
Jail at Springfield,	1	3	2	—	1	—	3	5
House of Correction, Springfield,	9	65	—	—	—	—	—	—
Jail at Northampton,	1	3	1	—	—	—	1	1
House of Correction, Northampton,	1	3	—	—	—	—	—	—
Jail at Cambridge,	1	3	—	—	—	—	—	—
House of Correction, Cambridge,	38	463	12	3	1	2	18	30
Jail at Lowell,	2	11	1	—	—	—	1	—
Jail at Dedham,	6	158	—	—	—	1	1	9

120 PRISONS AND PRISON DISCIPLINE. [Mar.

TABLE XVII.—*Sickness and Punishment in State, County, and City Prisons*—Concluded.

	Number of Sick discharged between March 1 and October ber 1, 1864.	Number of Days' Sickness.	Number who had been punished once.	Number who had been punished twice.	Number who had been punished three times.	Number who had been punished more than three times.	Whole number who had been punished.	Number of Punishments.
House of Correction, Dedham,	19	146	4	1	4	1	10	23
House of Correction, Plymouth,	1	3	1	—	1	—	2	4
House of Correction, Fitchburg,	3	30	4	2	1	3	10	37
House of Correction, Worcester,	9	68	14	4	—	3	21	39
Jail at Boston,	44	600	—	—	—	—	—	—
House of Correction, South Boston,	27	620	25	11	4	4	44	81
Totals for the County Prisons,	231	3,502	117	32	17	21	187	359
State Prison, Charlestown,	—	—	9	11	2	12	34	156
House of Reformation,* Deer Island,	10	47	2	4	3	6	15	51
House of Industry,* Deer Island,	251	633	10	4	1	—	15	21
Total for State and City Prisons,	261	670	21	19	6	18	64	228
Total for State, County and City Prisons,	492	4,172	138	51	23	39	251	587

* Since June 1st, 1864.

Expenses of Twenty-Four Prison Establishments.

Having given in the Annual Report the classified expenditures of the different County Prisons, I will here only exhibit them in the aggregate, together with the expenditures in the State Prison, and the two City Prisons* combined in a single establishment at Deer Island. It ought to be remembered, however, that the House of Reformation is a place of confinement for young offenders only, and that the sum expended there for instruction, (included in Salaries,) is upwards of a thousand dollars. This and the State Prison are the only ones to which women may not be sent; and girls are sent to the House of Reformation, though but few of them. The average number in this establishment, and in the House of Industry,— which is the Boston Workhouse,— is only approximate.

In entering these returns of expense, I have not attempted to reconcile the discrepancies, but have set down the figures as they came in. I presume the "total amount expended" is more likely to be correctly given than the classification by different items ; so that any apparent error should be reckoned an error in classification by the officers making the return. The net cost of all these prisons for the year ending September 30, 1864, appears to be $342,476.87 for about 2,010 prisoners; or an average weekly cost of about $3.27, exclusive of interest on the cost of the prisons, which would add between $1.75 and $2 a week more.

The salaries in these twenty-four establishments amount to $111,918.77 ; an average of nearly fifty-six dollars to each prisoner of the average number.

Whether we look at the results aimed at, or the amount of good actually done, the prisons would seem to be the least efficient of all our institutions in proportion to their expenses.†

---

* In speaking here and elsewhere of the House of Reformation as a *prison*, I do not mean to cast any reflection upon this long established and beneficent institution. In the eye of the law it is a prison, and its close connection with the House of Industry makes it impossible to draw a nice distinction.

† See Appendix D.

TABLE XVIII.—*Expenses of the State, County, and City Prisons, for the Year ending September 30, 1864.*

	Twenty-two County Prisons.	State Prison.	Deer Island Prison. House of Reformation and House of Industry.	Totals.
Salaries of Officers,	$71,686 55	$29,387 00	**$10,845 22	$111,918 77
Sum expended for Provisions,	81,014 57	23,635 30	33,437 89	138,087 76
Sum expended for Clothing,	9,233 38	*5,854 54	12,721 24	27,809 16
Sum expended for Fuel and Lights,	42,672 24	—	18,206 88	60,879 12
Sum expended for Beds and Bedding,	2,259 34	—	—	2,259 34
Sum expended for Medicine and Medical Attendance,	2,771 86	†204 99	669 72	3,441 58
Sum expended for Instruction of Prisoners,	3,545 09	‖457 80	—	3,750 08
Sum allowed to Discharged Prisoners,	908 68	—	35 25	1,401 73
Sum allowed to Witnesses,	11 40	—	—	11 40
Sum expended for all other purposes,	50,175 47	$24,072 61	36,921 69	111,169 77
Total amount expended,	236,775 49	83,612 24	112,837 89	433,225 62
Amount received for Labor of Prisoners,	34,339 28	¶56,208 07	201 40	90,748 75
Balance against the Prison,	202,436 21	27,404 17	112,636 49	342,476 87
Average Number of Prisoners,	1,133.5	376.66	††200 & 300††	2,010.16

* Includes "beds and bedding." † For library. ‖ Includes $91.84 paid for transportation of prisoners from jails.
§ Includes $1,363.11 for repairs and improvements. ¶ This sum includes $605.25 admission fees, and $579.87 for rents.
** House of Reformation, salaries, $2,967.13; House of Industry, salaries, $7,878.09. †† Approximate.

So great, and for such purposes have been the expenditures attending our system of imprisonment. But if we take into account the cost of the administration of criminal justice; the salaries of Judges, Solicitors, Sheriffs, Clerks, etc., the pay of Juries and witnesses, the fees of officers, the investment in Court Houses; and all that goes to swell the aggregate burden which crime and its punishment impose upon this Commonwealth and its people, we shall find that it amounts to no less than a million and perhaps a million and a half dollars by the year. That this heavy tax should be so expended as to diminish crime and improve the average morals of the community is the business of the General Court to provide. To allow crime to increase either wilfully or by indifference brings shame upon the magistrate, and suffering upon the people. Is it then asking too much of the Legislature of this Puritan Commonwealth to entreat your honorable body to investigate the whole subject of our penal and prison discipline, — to give it a place in your annual deliberations and finally establish such modifications as the facts of the case and the tendencies of the age require?

The high part which Massachusetts has been called to take in the tragic exigencies of the country, has been well filled; she has done more than any State to break the power of Slavery, and she has amply justified the legend on her shield. Sword in hand, she has sought peace through Liberty, and already begins to attain what she has sought. To adorn the repose of peace with its own trophies we must give renewed attention to those social questions of which the civil war has increased the gravity, while it has delayed the consideration. It is a good omen that in such a time the State has created a commission to investigate these questions, but the work of the Board of State Charities will be of little value unless seconded by the representatives of the people, to whom this imperfect Report is respectfully submitted.

F. B. SANBORN,
Secretary of the Board of State Charities.

Boston, February 15, 1865.

At a regular meeting of the Board of State Charities on Wednesday, March 1, 1865, it was voted,

"That the Secretary, having prepared the Report on Prisons contemplated in the vote of this Board, passed January 4, 1865, the same is hereby accepted, and the Secretary is directed to transmit the same to His Excellency the Governor."

A true copy,
  Attest,   F. B. SANBORN, *Secretary.*

APPENDIX.

[A.]

[See page 17.]

CAPTAIN MACONOCHIE AT NORFOLK ISLAND.

Alexander Maconochie, a Scotchman and sailor, was put in command of the penal colony on Norfolk Island, near Van Dieman's Land, in 1840. Some idea of his character, and the nature of his discipline, may be formed from the following passages written by himself, which I quote from Miss Carpenter's new book on Prison Discipline, entitled, "*Our Convicts.*"

He thus states the principles on which he worked, in a pamphlet published in Hobart Town, in 1839:—

"The example of severe suffering, consequent on conviction of crime, has not hitherto been found very effective in preventing its recurrence; and it seems probable that the example of *necessary reform*, or, at least, *sustained submission and self-command through a fixed period of probation*, before obtaining release from the restrictions in consequence of such correction, would be practically more so.

"The idea that would be thus presented would be more definite, more comprehensible, and more humbling to the false pride which usually attends the early practice of crime, and derives gratification at once from its successful perpetration, and from the bravado of thereby defying menaced *vindictive* punishment.

"And with reform, as the object of criminal administration, the better feeling of even the most abandoned criminals would from the beginning sympathize; whereas, when merely suffering and degradation are threatened and imposed, it is precisely these better feelings that both first and last are most revolted and injured by them.

"The sole direct object of secondary punishment should therefore, it is conceived, be the *reform*, if possible, but, at all events, the adequate subjugation and training to self-command of the individuals subjected to them; so that, before they can regain their full privileges in society, after once forfeiting them, they must give satisfactory proof that they again deserve and are not likely to abuse them.

"This principle does not proscribe *punishment, as such*, which, on the contrary, will, it is believed, be always found indispensable, in order to induce penitence and submission; nor, as may be already inferred, does it lose sight of the object of setting a deterring example. But it raises the character of both these elements in treatment, placing the first in the light of a *benevolent means*, whereas it is too often regarded as a *vindictive end*, and obtaining the second by the exhibition of the law *constantly and necessarily victorious over individual obstinacy*, instead of frequently defeated by it. It cannot be doubted that very much of the harshness and obduracy of old offenders arises at present from the gratified pride of having braved the worst that the law can inflict, and maintained an unconquerable will amidst all its severities; and for this pride there would be no place, if endurance alone could serve no useful end, and only submission could restore to freedom.

"The end *reform*, or its substitutes, sustained submission and self-command, being thus made the first objects of secondary punishments, it is next contended that they can only be adequately pursued and tested,—first, by dividing the process employed into specific *punishment for the past*, and specific *training for the future*, and next, by grouping prisoners together, in the latter stage, in associations made to resemble ordinary life as closely as possible (in particular, subdivided into smaller parties, or families, as may be agreed to among the men themselves, with common interests, and receiving wages in the form of marks of commendation, exchangeable at will for immediate gratifications, but of which a fixed accumulation should be required before the recovery of freedom,) thus preparing for society in society, and providing a field for the exercise and cultivation of active *social virtues*, as well as for the habitual *voluntary* restraint of active social vices."

These were the general principles on which Captain Maconochie founded his system. We learn how he developed them from a pamphlet he published on "Norfolk Island," in 1847, from which the following extracts are made:—

"I arrived at Norfolk Island," he says, "on the 6th of March, 1840, and found the state of things certainly not better, and in some respects even rather worse, than I had expected. Fourteen hundred doubly-convicted prisoners, the refuse of both penal colonies, (for the worst offenders were sent here from Van Dieman's Land as well as New South Wales,) were rigorously coerced all day, and cooped up at night in barracks which could not decently accommodate half that number. In every way their feelings were habitually outraged, and their self-respect destroyed.

"They were required to cap each private soldier whom they met, and even each empty sentry box that they passed. If they met a superior officer, they were to take off their caps altogether, and stand aside, bareheaded, in a ditch if necessary, and whatever the weather, till he passed, in most cases without taking the smallest notice of them.

"For the merest trifles they were flogged, ironed, or confined in jail for successive days on bread and water. * * * Neither knives nor forks, nor hardly any other conveniences, were allowed at their tables, They tore the food with their fingers and teeth, and drank for the most part out of water-buckets. Not more than about two-thirds of them could even enter their mess-shed at a time; and the rest, whatever the weather, were required to eat as they could in an open shed beside a large privy.

"The Island had been fifteen years a penal settlement when I landed, yet not a single place of worship was erected on it. It had been seven years a settlement, before even a clergyman was sent. There were no schools, no books; and the men's countenances reflected faithfully this description of treatment. A more demoniacal assemblage could not be imagined, and almost the most formidable sight I ever beheld was the sea of faces upturned to me when I first addressed them. Yet, three years afterwards, I had the satisfaction of hearing Sir George Gipps ask me what I had done to make the men look so well? he had seldom seen a better looking set; *they were quite equal to new prisoners from England.*

"It is impossible here to state in detail the means by which I accomplished this great change, indicating, as it did, other changes still greater and more important. Besides introducing most imperfectly my own system of management among them (for my marks never had a fixed value towards liberation, assigned them, which could alone make their accumulation really important,) I sought generally by every means to recover the men's self-respect, to gain their own wills towards their reform, to visit moral offences severely, but to reduce the number of those that were purely conventional, to mitigate the penalties attached to these, and thus gradually awaken better and more enlightened feelings among both officers and men. I built two churches, got a catechist added to the establishment to assist the chaplain,—almost every Sunday during all my four years, read the service myself, with a sermon, at some one or other out station,—established schools, distributed books, gave prizes for assiduity,—was unwearied myself in my counsels and exhortations, wherever I went, and went everywhere alone and unattended, showing confidence, and winning it in return. I also gave every man a small garden, which was a boon to the industrious, but none to the idle. Those whom I camped out in the bush, I encouraged also to rear pigs and poultry, thereby improving their ration, and, still more, infusing into them, by the possession of property, that instinctive respect for it which makes it safer in a community than any direct preservatives. I thus also interested my police, who were all prisoners, in the maintenance of order, their situations, which were much coveted, being made to depend on their success.

"I gave the messes knives, forks, a few cooking utensils, tin pannekins, &c. I allowed the overseers, police, and other first-class men to wear blue jackets and other articles of dress not portions of usual convict clothing; and nothing contributed more than this to raise their spirits, revive their self-respect, and confirm their good purposes.

"It has been alleged that I had no secret in my management except indulgence, and that the prisoners behaved well with me because they had all their own way. They little know prisoners who say this. Mere weakness never guided such men yet. They behaved well with me because they were reasoned with, not bullied, — because they were sought to be raised, not crushed, — because they had an interest in their own good conduct, — and because they knew that if, notwithstanding, they behaved ill, besides incurring the censure of their companions, they would be otherwise vigorously repressed. In individual cases, especially of moral offence, I was even more severe than any of my predecessors; and through the good spirit which I succeeded in infusing into the mass, I obtained evidence in such cases when no one else ever had.

"It has been said, too, that many of my results were owing to my own personal influence, and I willingly admit this to have been great; but it must have terminated when the men left the Island; and yet what are the undoubted facts as to their conduct then? In four years I discharged 920 doubly convicted men to Sydney, of whom only 20, or 2 per cent., had been re-convicted up to January, 1845, the latest period to which I have any returns. Of 538, whom I discharged to Van Dieman's Land in February, 1844, sixteen months afterwards, viz., in July, 1845, only 15, or under 3 per cent., were under punishment; by which, I understand, had committed grave offences. [See Return, No. 36, Commons Papers, 1846, p. 57.] At the same time, the proportion of Van Dieman's Land trained men, in the same circumstances, was 888 out of 10,365, or 9 per cent. (same Papers, p. 54;) and in England, France, and Belgium, during the last five years, the proportion of discharged prisoners re-convicted, has varied from 33 to 35 per cent., while in Middlesex and Lancashire it was, last year, 47 per cent.; and among men discharged from the general prison at Perth, a separate prison of the most improved construction, during the last four years, it has been 67 per cent.

"Much is currently said of the necessary demoralization attending the association of prisoners together; and I readily admit that if, on the usual principles of management, only their worst feelings are called out, their accumulation cannot but aggravate the evil. But if we will bring their better impulses into play instead, — and it is quite easy to do this by proper combinations, without sacrificing any portion of reasonable punishment, — then prisoners will be found just like other men. They are born social beings, so fashioned by the hand of their Creator; and it is in society, the society of their equals, not in seclusion from it, or in exclusive contact with superiors, that their most valuable qualities will infallibly be called out.

"In dealing with prisoners we habitually make a variety of mistakes, . each more important than another, yet to which professed disciplinarians are all zealously attached. We draw no proper distinction between moral and merely conventional offences. By minute regulations we multiply the number of these latter, and at the same time exaggerate their importance. We thus wear out the spirits and exhaust the feelings of obedience and subordination in our men by incessant demands on them, for pure frivolities. We also sear their consciences by familiarizing them in this way with petty offences. We trust altogether to force to compass our ends. We seek to bend men like oziers, or to cast them, as we would dough, in stone moulds. We allow the higher principles of human nature to lie dormant in our prisons; we afford no scope for their exercise; we make no appeal but to immediate submission; we give no charge to men of their own destiny; we keep them as automata in our hands; and having thus done everything in our power to weaken them, we look to make up for our blunders by placing them afterwards in 'favorable circumstances.' Is this a school of virtue, or of pure dandling? Is not the whole process an absurdity? *Nitimur in adversum* is the real road to improvement; and we give our prisoners neither opportunity for making this manly struggle, nor the chance of acquiring energy and independence of character through its means. We make them look and act exclusively to order while in our hands, and we wonder and exclaim at their perverseness when they afterwards fall, through the weakness that we have ourselves induced.

"The system that I advocate avoids all these errors, and does not, I think, fall into any others worth naming. It may be improved in its details, but I doubt if any of its principles can be advantageously dispensed with. It seeks to grant no weak or unmeaning indulgences; but it desires to gain soul as well as body — to influence, and not merely coerce.

"It draws the line of duty under the guidance of religion and morality, not of conventional regulation. It seeks to punish criminals by placing them in a position of severe adversity, from which only long-sustained effort and self-denial can extricate them; but it does not desire to aggravate this position by unworthy scorn, or hatred, or contempt; and, on the contrary, it respects our common nature, however temporarily fallen or alienated. It does not encourage a man, approaching his freedom, by an abatement of task, or improvement of diet, — the low rewards of existing low systems, — which flatter the spirit of self-indulgence, that leads most criminals to their first fall; but it at once proves and stimulates, and cheers him on, by an increasing and ever increasing scope of free agency, with motives to guide it, yet not unmingled with difficulty to resist its temptations. And seeking thus to train men for discharge into any circumstances, it is not afraid of being able to qualify them for even the most difficult.

"Nothing could be more unfavorable than my position on Norfolk Island, for conducting a great and moral experiment; and yet, guided by these principles, none could easily be more successful. Of all stations in the Penal Colonies this was confessedly the most demoralized. My powers in it were limited. My immediate superior, Sir George Gipps, only partially convinced of the soundness of my views, frequently hesitated, and not unfrequently even refused to support me in them. My machinery on the Island was raw. Much of it was theoretical even in my own mind; and being the development of a new idea, some mistakes were probably unavoidable in its first organization. My officers were not all cordial in their support of me; trained in the previous system, it was difficult to induce them to look with favor on one which shocked so many old prejudices, which by raising the prisoner lowered the relative *status* of the free man; and which, by compelling private work to be paid for, diminished many long-established advantages. My marks, also, never had the only value given them, that towards liberation, which could make their accumulation an object of steady pursuit to the men. My physical means were always deficient. I never had above 160 soldiers in garrison with me, instead of from 200 to 300, who have since been maintained there. I had only five inferior free officers engaged in the active business of the establishment, instead of from 20 to 30, who have since been attached to it. And my police and overseers were selected by myself from the ordinary prisoners, instead of being free or probationers, as since sent from the mother colony.

"Yet, amidst all these disadvantages, the moral means employed by me were fully equal to their task. I found the Island a turbulent, brutal hell, and I left it a peaceful, well-ordered community. Almost the first words of Sir George Gipps' report on it (in spite of some strong previous impressions in his mind against my plans,) are:—'Notwithstanding that my arrival was altogether unexpected, I found good order everywhere to prevail, and the demeanor of the prisoners to be respectful and quiet.' Besides this, the most complete security, alike of person and property, prevailed. Officers, women, and children traversed the Island everywhere without fear; and huts, gardens, stock-yards, and growing crops—many of them, as of fruit, most tempting—were scattered in every corner without molestation. I confess that I have since looked back even with wonder at the scene, familiar as it then was to me. There were flaws in the picture, doubtless, but they were fewer and more minute than, without tracing the causes, may easily be believed.

" My task was not really so difficult as it appeared. I was working *with* Nature, and not against her, as all other prison systems do. I was endeavoring to cherish, and yet direct and regulate, those cravings for amelioration of position which almost all possess, in some degree, and which are often strongest in those otherwise the most debased. Under the guidance of right principle, they rose with me easily to order and exertion, while, under mere control, they not unfrequently either explode in violence, or, being crushed, drag the whole man down with them. I looked to them for success, and in them I found it. I did not neglect the object of *punishment* in my various arrangements; but I sought it within the limits assigned alike by the letter and spirit of the law, not by excesses of authority beyond them. The law imposes *imprisonment* and *hard labor* as a retribution for offence; and these, in the fullest sense of the words, my men endured. Every one of them performed his government task, besides the labor that he bestowed, as he could catch an opportunity, on his garden or other interests. But he was saved, as far as I could save him, from unnecessary humiliation, and encouraged to look to his own steady efforts for ultimate liberation and improved position. And this, not the efforts of an individual, zealous as they doubtless were, was the real secret of the altered aspect of Norfolk Island in my time, from what either preceded or followed it."

" The Mark System," he continues, " proposes to place criminals in a state of utter poverty, destitution, and bondage, from which nothing but their own steady, persevering, unflinching exertion can eradicate them. They are to be at the bottom of a well, with a ladder provided by which they *may* ascend if they *will*, but without any bolstering or dragging up by other than their own efforts. If they even halt they are made to descend, for their maintenance from day to day is to be charged to them. Are these not here, then, sufficient elements of suffering to produce a deterring effect? yet everything is strictly conducive to reform; and why, therefore, go further?

" Why introduce, in addition, chains, and dungeons, and factitious offences, and all the other apparatus of slavery, so much clung to in ordinary prison discipline, yet so injurious alike to officers and men? Why stigmatize that system as over indulgent which merely ejects these, while substituting at the same time far harder conditions to a degraded mind than they constituted?

"A fallen spirit can easily put up with a little more degradation, a little more contumely, a few harsh restrictions which there is always a contemplated pleasure in evading; to set his shoulder to the wheel, steadily to struggle out of his position, to command his temper, his appetites, his self-indulging propensities, all voluntarily, all from an *inward* impulse stimulated by a moral necessity, this is a far harder imposition." * * * * * *

"My intellectual apparatus, I propose uniformly, for the express purpose of awakening, stimulating, and keeping the mind active, as well as the body; storing it, at the same time, with better thoughts than the disgusting images otherwise most familiar to prisoners; and in this light they cannot be too highly valued. It is in the intervals of entire repose, which, in ordinary management, are allowed to alternate with severe physical toil, that such men corrupt each other. My music, readings aloud, schools, novels, and other similar machinery, then kept many a devil out, and, perhaps, introduced some angels in. They were negatively beneficial at all events, and, I feel assured, in very many cases, positively beneficial also."

Another part of his system, to which he attached great importance, was the cultivation among the prisoners of a mutual dependence and interest in each others' welfare.

This he found peculiar difficulties in developing as he desired.

"Alone, unassisted," he continues, "pursuing a previously untrodden path, on a voyage of discovery rather than guided by positive knowledge, without a precedent, and anxious, by yielding some points to those around me, to gain others, I relaxed in this, which gave both my officers and men extra trouble, *and suffered for it accordingly.* There is no part of my whole system to which I am now more attached, though I readily admit its early practical difficulties.

"The men themselves will never, in the first instance, like it, though they speedily accommodate themselves to, and are benefited by it. Very few of my parties practically separated, even when released by their advance to tickets-of-leave, from its imperative obligations. It was rather a reproach to them when they did. All, in a degree, lost caste when a hut-party broke up.

"And some very remarkable instances of the most disinterested self-sacrifice were elicited, while the sentiments which they indicated were, in a degree, implanted through this means. * * * Under the mark system the criminals come in selfish, unwilling to trouble themselves about their companions, desirous only of ease, and evasion, and self-indulgence, and thus ready to fall into all those horrors incident to prisoners under the present management; but, under the strong impulse afforded by the system, they gradually become social, generous, active, and well-purposed throughout. 'They wash, and are cleansed.' Religiously, I repeat it, they may not be converted.

"In this respect too many of us all are as Ethiopians and leopards, and may not change our skins or cast our spots. But even in this respect, many may come through their temporal good to see also their spiritual; and it is beyond all contradiction that a *right agency* will make improved social agents of even the worst; or, if this is considered doubtful, it will be time enough to pronounce authoritatively to such effect *when a right agency shall have been for some time tried.* That period is certainly not yet arrived."

At the time Captain Machonochie took charge of Norfolk Island he was fifty-three years old; and he had spent the greater part of these years in a rough life among sailors and soldiers. For two or three years he was a prisoner of war at Verdun in France, and so had learned by experience what imprisonment is.

He was recalled from Norfolk Island in 1844; and the old system of cruelty was re-established there, ending as it had before 1840, in mutiny and murder.

In 1849 he was appointed Governor of the Birmingham Jail, but was removed in 1851, by magistrates who misunderstood his system. He died about four years ago,—that is, on the 25th of October, 1860.

[B.]

[See page 56.]

PRISON LABOR IN EUROPE.

In the European prisons, generally speaking, the labor of prisoners has been far less remunerative than in this country, where for more than thirty years great pains have been taken to make State Prisons self-supporting, as in many States of the Union they have been. In Massachusetts this was the case between the years 1830 and 1854, or nearly a quarter of a century; the profit of that period equalling the expense of the prison. Of late years, while our State Prison has been growing more costly, (having incurred in the last eleven years a deficit of over $130,000,) the European prisons have been growing more remunerative, except in England. From a recent address of Sir John Bowring, well known as a man of learning and of affairs, I gather the following particulars relating to the subject, which are of later date than my own researches afford:—

"In France the plan of the absolute isolation of prisoners by day was abandoned in 1848, and a classified system of employment was introduced. In all the central and departmental prisons the areas were turned into workshops, and with some modifications the arrangements which had been successfully carried out in the United States prisons— and in which the recommittals were not six per cent.—were adopted, and the system gradually extended to the sale of the productions of the prisoners to contractors, under the prison regulations. Upon the introduction of the contract system the yearly receipts from that source derived from the nineteen central prisons was £12,000 per annum; in 1862 it was £47,000, and the profit from the whole of that year amounted to no less a sum than £121,000. Of this sum proportions varying from one-tenth to six-tenths were allowed to different classes of prisoners; a portion of the sum having been distributed amongst them during their confinement, and the rest having been allowed to accumulate, was handed to them at the time of their liberation. As far as practicable the convicts were employed at the trades to which they had been brought up. Saddlers returned the greatest profit; the next most profitable were the shoemakers, then the tailors, basket-makers, mat-makers, and the stone-cutters and weavers. In a report lately made to the French Legislature by M. Jules Simon, it was stated that under the beneficent influences of the new system, the number of prisoners had diminished one-half, and that in one of the departments the prison had twice been without a single occupant."

In Belgium results still more satisfactory have been obtained:—

"As regarded the importance of remunerative prison labor, a body of commissioners who reported upon it to the Belgian House of Representatives, expressed a most decided opinion that it was a powerful and needful agent in reforming criminals, that it checked recommittals, and provided against misery, and they quoted approvingly the words of M. Bérenger to the French Chamber of Peers, that whatever be the character of the imprisonment to which a criminal is condemned, labor must be the basis of all moral improvement, and its employment a necessity from which it is impossible to escape. The report stated that the produce of the labor on an average of three years was £16,350, of which more than three-fourths was work for the army, or for the use of the prisons. The six central prisons of Belgium left a profit from labors of £20,000, of which £1,600 was distributed in rewards. The maximum term required for learning the trade of shoemaking was twelve months, weaving six months, tailoring three months. In a return to the Minister of Justice, giving the receipts and expenditure of the Antwerp prison, in which all the convicts were employed in manufacturing stuffs for exportation, it was shown that in twelve years the quantity produced was to the value of £400,000—the greater part of the productions were made of raw materials, the growth of Belgium, and of which the native agricultural industry had the benefit; and the report prided itself on the fact that the capital of remote nations had thus contributed to the reform of Belgian criminals and to the finances of the Belgian State. The return for the period named exhibited a net profit of £29,400, being an annual average of £2,450. For the last year it had been £3,240. The number of prisoners was 1,295."

If by net profit is here meant a profit over and above the whole expenses of the prison, the result would be almost identical with that mentioned as existing at the Albany Penitentiary. Whether this is the case I cannot say.

Since preparing the statistics of the Albany Penitentiary, the annual report of that institution for 1864 has been received, from which the following statement of the year's income and expenditures is obtained. Income for 1864:—

From Shoe Shop,	$30,150	12
Female Department,	3,997	30
Board Account,	19,457	38
Visitors and Fines,	321	64
Total Income,	$53,926	44

Total Income brought forward,		$53,926 44
Expenditures for 1864:—		
For Improvements and Repairs,	$725 19	
Furniture,	700 87	
Clothing and Bedding,	3,141 32	
Provisions,	15,202 07	
Building Account,	5,201 54	
General Expense Account,	13,781 54	
Total Expenses,		38,752 53
Gain to the Institution,		$15,173 91

Sir John Bowring also spoke of the prisons of Switzerland and Spain, which gave a profit per head, and furnished an instance of 2,355 prisoners having been taught in a Spanish jail to earn an honest livelihood. Forty workshops had been erected there without cost to the Government by the labor of the prisoners. An English traveller, Mr. Hoskins, called the result "a miracle," and inquired why similar experiments were not carried out in this country. The want was co-operation on the part of the Government. The Bavarian Government had established five agricultural and industrial prisons, whose working was spoken of as most satisfactory, and as having produced a considerable diminution of recommittals. The prison of Katchvain, in Thurgovia, received the vagabonds of most of the adjacent Swiss cantons, and paid all its expenses by the produce of labor without any State assistance, and in the canton of Friburg the profits of labor amounted to £1,200 from 110 prisoners, that is £10 per head, more than nine-tenths of which were produced by labor in the open air.

The Spanish prison here referred to is no doubt that at Valencia, which I have described.

Sir John Bowring contrasts with these statistics those of the Devon County gaol, where 216 prisoners earned £47 13s. 3d., or about one dollar apiece. This is almost as bad as our Norfolk County prison, where 75 prisoners earn nothing.

[C.]

[See page 64.]

WHAT IS MEANT BY RECOMMITMENTS.

The word *recommitment* or *recommittal* is used in several ways, and much confusion often arises from a clear distinction between these. I use it in the sense of the *imprisonment of a person who has previously been confined in any prison;* excluding, of course, all reference to the preliminary confinement which preceded conviction. But in the statistics of the State Prison, the custom seems to be to class as recommitments only those cases where the person has been previously committed to that particular prison; and, as I have no means of going beyond these statistics, wherever I have mentioned the State Prison recommitments, they must be taken with this allowance. Of course *all* persons sent to Charlestown under sentence have been previously confined in the county jail, or some other prison, pending trial and sentence, but this we do not take into the account. Many of them, also, have been previously under suspicion or sentence in the county prisons; this fact, however, does not appear. I can understand that the proportion of previously imprisoned persons at Charlestown should be less than at South Boston or New Bedford, but I cannot believe it is less than in the average of the county prisons.

With respect to the great number of recommitments to jails and houses of correction, it should be said that this cannot be supposed exaggerated in the returns. In many cases, it depends upon the statement of the prisoner himself, who is more likely to deny than admit a previous commitment; in other cases it is decided by the recollections of the prison officer, or the records of the prison, which would generally exclude previous commitments *to any other prison;* and there are comparatively few instances in which an error would be likely to occur increasing the true number of commitments. It may, therefore, be assumed as certain, I think, that the recorded number of recommitments not only is not above, but is considerably below the truth.

As to the precise character of these recommitments, and how far our prison system is responsible for them, opinions will differ. It is doubtless true that many of them are fine and cost cases, where drunkenness is the offence, and where the time of imprisonment is too short to allow any prison discipline an opportunity to benefit the persons in question. Among the females many of them are prostitutes—a class whose reformation is very difficult under any circumstances, and who can hardly be expected to profit much by any prison discipline, unless it is long

continued, and followed by close supervision after discharge. It is stated by Judge Pitman, formerly of the New Bedford Police Court, that these women greatly dread the House of Correction, and are glad to be sent to the workhouse instead, where they pass the winter without severe labor, are reëstablished in health, and are ready to go out in spring to their shameful vocation, entirely unaffected by punishment or attempted reformation. With regard to these two classes—drunkards among men and prostitutes among women,—the blame of their frequent recommitment must rest mainly upon our penal code, which establishes unreasonably slight or ill-suited penalties.

But the recommitments for larceny, and many other crimes, especially those committed by the young, are directly traceable to the imperfections of our prison system, which, as is well known to all who have had much acquaintance with it, does little to reform and much to corrupt these offenders. If this were merely my own opinion, I should hesitate to express it so strongly; but I have consulted magistrates and prison officers of long experience, who declare that this view of the matter entirely agrees with their own, and I have found no person who after examination, materially dissents from it.

There is a third method of reckoning recommitments which seems to be used in Ireland, and which Captain Maconochie and Colonel Montesinos appear to have used; namely, to reckon the proportion of relapses among discharged prisoners. That is, out of one thousand prisoners discharged from Norfolk Island, or Valencia, a certain number will be again imprisoned. These are called recommitments, and the percentage of them is calculated on the whole number *discharged*, instead of the whole number *committed*. This is the best test of a prison system, provided all the cases could be reported; but in this country it would be impossible to apply it with any accuracy. It is this test which we seek to apply to our reform schools, where it is far easier to do so; but even there, no very satisfactory statistics can be obtained.

These remarks have been made to anticipate the criticism of having used a shifting and deceptive term in my calculations. I think it will appear that the facts in the case really warrant stronger condemnation of our prison system and our penal law than I have felt at liberty to make. My object has been to state facts and arouse the public attention, not to excite prejudice.

[D.]

[See page 121.]

OUR PRISON EXPENSES.

In stating the expenditures of the county prisons for 1864 in the Annual Report, I compared them with the expenses as reported for ten years preceding. It will, perhaps, be said, that during the years preceding 1859, when the prison officers were allowed certain fees, and boarded their prisoners on their own risk for $1.75 a week, the reported expenses do not give any just view of the real cost of the prisons, especially in the matter of salaries. This is partially true, but having no other authority than the annual returns, I have been obliged to use those. But it is the common belief (well founded, as I suppose,) that at the time when only $1.75 was allowed for the weekly board of prisoners, the officers who supplied them found it very profitable to do so. This would show that the true weekly cost of their support must have been less than half what it now is.

As to salaries, it is further to be remembered that many of the reported salaries include in addition the board of the officers, sometimes of his family, and always larger or smaller perquisites attaching to the place. In addition to this, there is, in some counties, great political influence implied in the position of a prison officer disposed to exercise it. The evil effects of such exercise, on a large scale, can be seen in New York, where the State Prisons are managed notoriously in the interest of parties and politicians. On a smaller scale our own local elections illustrate the same evil, which should be checked by legislation, if possible. It was a fortunate prudence on the part of our people to keep the appointment of judges where the constitution originally placed it, and if the choice of sheriffs could be restored to the same hands, or even made to take place at the spring elections, when it would be somewhat withdrawn from the vortex of State and National politics, the administration of justice, and the discipline of prisons would be improved thereby.

AN INDEX BY TOPICS.

	Page.
Special Message of Governor Andrew,	4
Introduction,	6
PART FIRST. — THE VARIOUS SYSTEMS OF PRISON DISCIPLINE,	7–52
I. The English Convict System,	9–16
(1.) Penal Servitude and Tickets-of-Leave,	10
(2.) Prisons and Prison Labor,	11
(3.) Prison Discipline,	13
(4.) The Ticket-of-Leave,	14
(5.) Convicts sent to Western Australia,	15
(6.) Juvenile and Female Offenders,	15
II. The Irish Convict System,	16–33
(1.) The Irish Prisons and Prison Labor,	18
(2.) The Mark System, Gratuities, etc.,	19
(3.) The Intermediate Prisons,	21
Smithfield,	21
Lusk,	23
Lectures to Prisoners,	24
(4.) The Irish Ticket-of-Leave,	24
(5.) Employment of Discharged Prisoners,	26
(6.) Police Supervision,	28
Supervision in the Country,	31
(7.) Female Convicts and Female Refuges,	32
III. The Parliamentary Commission of 1863,	33–36
IV. The two Systems of England and Ireland compared,	36–46
(1.) Intermediate Prisons,	38
(2.) Police Supervision,	39
(3.) Results of the Two Systems,	40
(a.) England,	40
(b.) Ireland,	41
(4.) Comparative Expense of the Two Systems,	44
(5.) Recent Legislation,	45
V. The Spanish Convict System,	46–49
VI. The Bavarian Convict System,	49–52
VII. The General Tendency of Prison Reform in Europe,	52

INDEX.   141

		Page.
PART SECOND. — THE MASSACHUSETTS SYSTEM AND ITS RESULTS,		53
I.	Great Increase in the Cost of County Prisons,	53
II.	The Albany Penitentiary,	55
III.	The Expense of our Jails,	62
IV.	Labor in the House of Correction,	62
V.	Our Prisons do not diminish Crime,	63
VI.	Our Prisons considered as Schools of Reform,	65
VII.	Four Tests of our System,	66
VIII.	Classifications and Conditional Remissions,	67
IX.	Habitual Criminals,	68
X.	Classification must be thorough,	69
XI.	The Instruction of Prisoners,	71
XII.	Discharged Prisoners,	74
XIII.	Increase of Crime among Females and Minors,	75
XIV.	The Nativity, Temperance, etc., of our Prisoners,	80
XV.	Summary of Suggestions,	82
	I. Penal Discipline,	82
	II. Prison Discipline,	82
PART THIRD. — PRISON STATISTICS OF MASSACHUSETTS FOR 1864,		85
Table IX.	Date, Cost, etc., County Prisons,	86–88
X.	Commitments,	90–91
XI.	Classification of Prisoners in the State,	94–95
XII.	Classification of Crimes in the State,	96–97
XIII.	Classification of Discharges for the State,	98–99
XIV.	Classification of Prisoners — County Prisons,	100–105
XV.	Classification of Crimes — County Prisons,	106–111
XVI.	Classification of Discharges — County Prisons,	112–117
XVII.	Sickness and Punishments,	119–120
XVIII.	Expenses of Twenty-Four Prisons,	122
APPENDIX—		
A.	Captain Maconochie at Norfolk Island,	125–133
B.	Prison Labor in Europe,	134–136*
C.	What is meant by Recommitments,	137–138
D.	Our Prison Expenses,	139
Index,		140

Printed in Dunstable, United Kingdom

82202395R00080